ARIZONA HIGHWAYS

HIKING GUIDE

52 OF ARIZONA'S BEST DAY HIKES FOR WINTER, SPRING, SUMMER & FALL

BY ROBERT STIEVE

Text: ROBERT STIEVE
Photographs: *ARIZONA HIGHWAYS* CONTRIBUTORS AND STAFF
Designer/Creative Director: BARBARA GLYNN DENNEY
Photo Editor: JEFF KIDA
Maps: KEVIN KIBSEY
Editorial Assistant: MARYAL MILLER
Copy Editor: BETH DEVENY

Library of Congress Control Number: 2010913750
ISBN 978-0-9845709-2-8
First and second printing, 2011. Printed in China.

Published by the Book Division of *Arizona Highways* magazine,
a monthly publication of the Arizona Department of Transportation,
2039 W. Lewis Avenue, Phoenix, Arizona 85009.
Telephone: 602-712-2200
Website: www.arizonahighways.com

Publisher: WIN HOLDEN
Editor: ROBERT STIEVE
Senior Editor/Books: RANDY SUMMERLIN
Managing Editor: KELLY KRAMER
Creative Director: BARBARA GLYNN DENNEY
Design Production Assistant: DIANA BENZEL-RICE
Photography Editor: JEFF KIDA
Production Director: MICHAEL BIANCHI
Production Assistant: ANNETTE PHARES

WARNING: Hiking on Arizona's trails, in a wide variety of environments, involves some physical risk. Each hiker has to make a personal decision about assuming those risks. Many of the hikes in this book are long and arduous. Weather can be a factor, along with wildlife and the physical condition and backcountry knowledge of the hiker. The author has attempted to provide accurate information about each hike. Users of this guide are urged to obtain full information and skills to undertake a hike. The author and publisher disclaim any liability for injury or other loss or damage incurred during any of these hikes or activities.

Front Cover: Jenn Hoffman and Scott Shapiro hike on the Mogollon Rim. | **NICK BEREZENKO**

WINTER HIKES

NICK BEREZENKO

SPRING HIKES

DEREK VON BRIESEN

SUMMER HIKES

NICK BEREZENKO

FALL HIKES

TOM BEAN

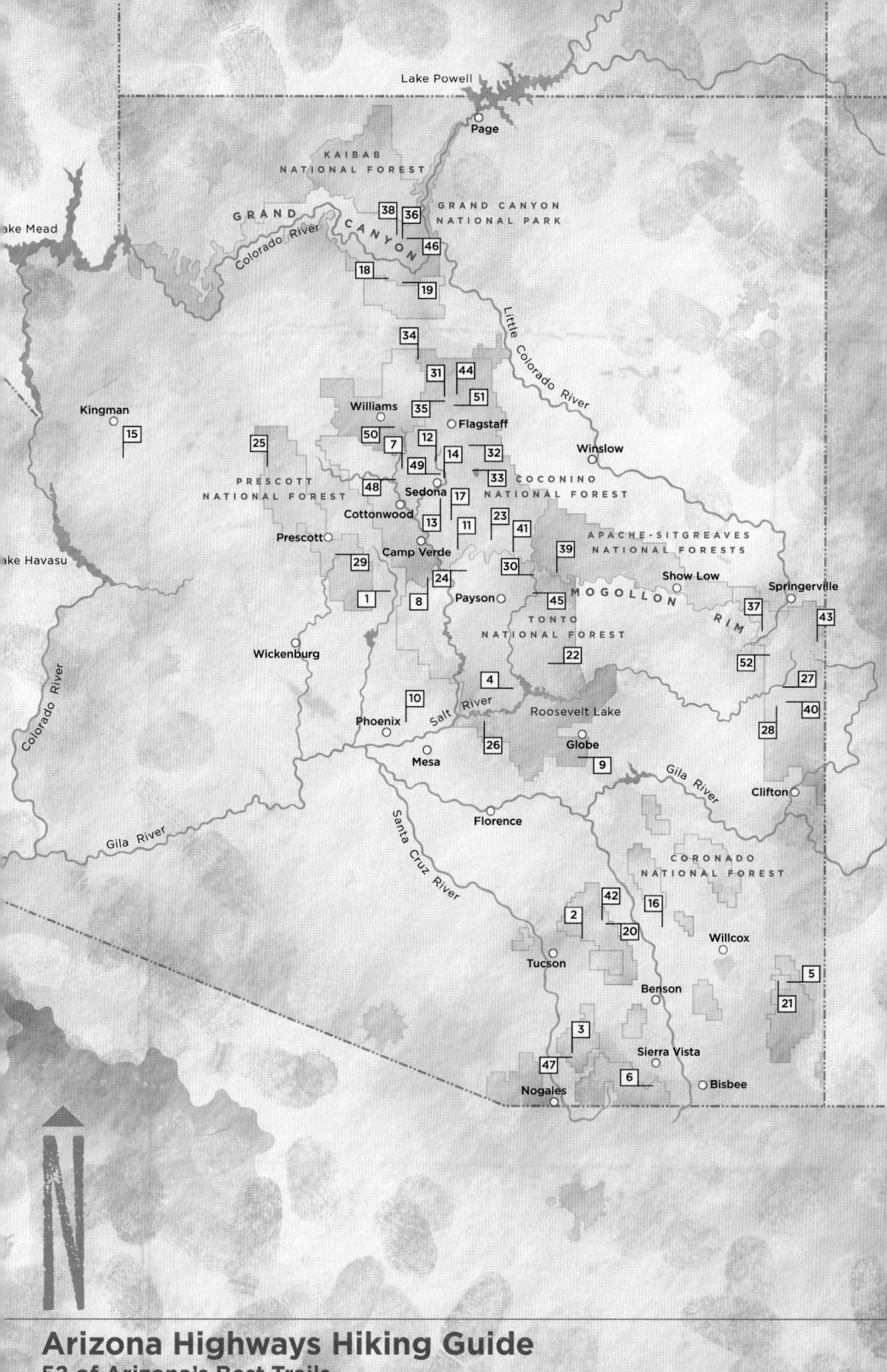

Arizona Highways Hiking Guide

52 of Arizona's Best Trails

y grandmother promised me she'd live long enough to read this book. She was in her late 80s at the time, and she was matter-of-factly planning the rest of her life. She didn't make it. After nine decades of writing and inspiring me to do the same, she couldn't wait any longer. I regret that she's not around to read my book. She wasn't much of a hiker in her later years, but she was pleased that her passion for the written word had trickled down the family tree, and she would have pored over every word — putting her in a small group that includes our proofreaders, a few staffers who had no choice, and a desperate insomniac in East Lansing, Michigan.

She would also have been unequivocally critical, questioning my word choices, the use of sentence fragments and split infinitives, the general lack of semicolons, and the list goes on. Her voice and her writing style were very different from mine, and our conversations could be painfully blunt at times, but I learned from her, and she inspired me to do what I do for a living, which includes writing hiking books.

If you're into the great outdoors, you know there are dozens of local hiking books available, and many of them are excellent. What sets this book apart is the street credibility of *Arizona Highways*. Like our iconic magazine, this book features the photography of the world's most respected landscape photographers — Nick Berezenko, Jack Dykinga, Suzanne Mathia, David Muench, Randy Prentice, et al. — as well as the spectacular fine art of our resident mapmaker, Kevin Kibsey. It's also unique because of its composition. This is the only hiking book in Arizona that's arranged according to the four seasons.

The Green Mountain Trail (see page 102) in the Santa Catalina Mountains offers hikers a cool escape from the desert heat. | JACK DYKINGA

Because of the state's geographical diversity, hiking is a year-round activity in Arizona — desert trails in the winter, mountain trails in the summer, and everything else somewhere in between. There are a lot of hikes out there, and our book features 52 of the best — one for each weekend of the year, sorted by seasons. Of course, many of the trails in Arizona are doable over multiple seasons, and some can even be done year-round. Our lineup is simply a guideline to get you started. It's not meant to be an absolute.

Likewise, this book is not intended to be a scientific journal. I'm pretty good with rocks and trees and birds in the sky, which I reference throughout, but this wasn't written for bird-watchers or botanists. It was written for anyone who feels the need to get off the couch once in a while, whether that's an extreme athlete looking for altitude or a casual hiker in need of a nature walk. What's more, it's driven by the words of John Muir, who wrote: "Climb the mountains and get their good tidings. Nature's peace will flow into you as sunshine flows into trees. The winds will blow their own freshness into you, and the storms their energy, while cares will drop off like autumn leaves."

If you can relate to what Mr. Muir is saying, you'll find some value in the following pages, which feature 52 of my favorite trails, 51 of which are straightforward day hikes. The exception is the Bright Angel Trail, which runs for nearly 10 miles from the South Rim of the Grand Canyon to the Colorado River. Although the National Park Service warns against doing this as a one-day excursion, I've done it many times, and so have thousands of others. You can do it as a day hike, but before you hit the trail, you'll have to gauge your own abilities and make an informed decision.

The only other hike that comes with a disclaimer is the Barbershop Trail. With the other hikes in this book, getting to the trailhead is the only step that requires any navigational prowess — once you're there, the trails are easy to follow. The Barbershop is different. You'll need to be more Magellan than Mr. Magoo on that hike, but if you pay attention and follow the written instructions, you'll be fine. More than anything, common sense is imperative on the trail. Always pack a thinking cap, and always adhere to the basic rules. Here are my top 10:

1. Never hike alone.
2. Tell someone where you're hiking, the route you'll be taking and when you'll be home.
3. Carry identification (driver's license, etc.) and the name and telephone number of whom to call in case of emergency.
4. Before you leave home, check the forecast, and pay attention to the weather while you're on the trail.
5. Study the maps before you go, and carry a compass, not just a GPS.
6. On the trail, know where you're going and where you are in relation to the map you're carrying.
7. Take plenty of food and carry more water than you think you'll need.
8. There's no such thing as too much sunscreen.
9. Don't overestimate your abilities.
10. Adhere to the Leave No Trace principles (see page 19).

Those 10 commandments are spelled out in more detail in the book's introduction, and although some of the rules might seem obvious or over-the-top, you never know what you'll encounter on the trail. For me, the unexpected first occurred on the Parsons Trail. It was the third trail of the 52 I'd write about for this book, and I was trekking with Kelly Kramer, our associate editor. As trails go, Parsons is one of the easiest. There's very little elevation change, and the trail itself is mostly sand and smooth dirt. Nonetheless, about 2 miles in, I stepped up onto a rock, heard a loud pop and felt a sharp pain. I hadn't slipped or tripped or turned an ankle, but somehow I managed to rupture my right calf muscle.

Fortunately, Kelly was there — Rule No. 1: Never hike alone. Because she was 4 months pregnant and half my size, she wasn't much help in carrying me out, but she did help me assess the situation and convince me to turn around — Rule No. 9: Don't overestimate your abilities. Eventually, after hopping out for 2 miles on my good leg, we made it to the ER in Cottonwood. From there, Kelly drove us back to Phoenix and I began 3 months of physical rehab in Scottsdale. A year later, on the anniversary of the accident, Kelly and I went back and finished the hike.

As it turns out, there are some other hikes I'll have to do again. In all, I did about 10 hikes that didn't make it into print. In some cases they were nixed because the access roads were too rough or the trails were too hard to follow, or in the case of the Hinkle Springs Trail, it was bagged because the trailhead is located on a private ranch. Forest fires and snowstorms put the kibosh on some trails, as well. There were dozens of fits and starts along the way, but overall, writing this book was an incredible adventure without any dull moments.

In addition to the ruptured calf muscle and a subsequent ruptured eardrum, I went through three pairs of Lowa hiking boots, two pairs of Maui Jim sunglasses and 52 bags of whole-grain Goldfish crackers. I changed three flat tires, dodged a rockslide on the Parsons Trail and found a half-empty helium balloon with a child's note tied to it on the Hell's Hole Trail. I trudged through 8-foot snowdrifts on the Pine Mountain Trail, hiked nearly 50 miles on the Arizona Trail, waded through the icy, chest-deep waters of Oak Creek in early spring, and saw two beautiful women in bikinis near Seven Falls in the dead of winter. I saw wildlife, too, including black bears, elk, pronghorns, mule deer, Coues white-tailed deer, bighorn sheep, coyotes, bobcats, javelinas, turkeys, Kaibab squirrels, Abert's squirrels, antelope squirrels, raccoons, coatimundis, a Mohave green rattlesnake and four of his cousins. I watched an owl and a skunk tussle for nearly an hour in the Galiuro Mountains — in the end, neither one of them won, or maybe both of them did. I also saw birds galore, but no elegant trogons, and I saw just about every tree that grows in Arizona, including an old sycamore in Ramsey Canyon that dates back to 1760. I saw a lot from the trail, and so will you.

In my case, most of those experiences were shared with friends and family, and I'd like to thank everyone who skipped work, tagged along and kept me company: Adam, Allison, Amy, Beth, Jackson, Kelly, Leah, Lexi, Lily, Maryal, Molly, Skip and Susan. Writing a hiking book is good work if you can get it, but it was even better with all of you at my side. I'll be curious to hear your feedback on the trails we trekked together — yes, you're obligated to read this book. Just don't say anything about my word choices or the use of sentence fragments. Even though she didn't live long enough to read this book, I can still hear my grandmother saying: "Do you really think 'cacophony' was the best word to use in that sentence? And what do you have against semicolons?"

— Robert Stieve

USING THIS GUIDEBOOK

Each hike in this book includes a trail description, a map, an interesting tidbit (*Foot Note*) and a Trail Guide. The latter offers a quick reference to the most important details. Here's a breakdown of what's included in each of the Trail Guides:

LENGTH

The length for each hike is listed as a round-trip distance, measured in miles. However, in the description of each trail, distances are measured primarily in minutes. That's because most people aren't adept at gauging mileage as they're chugging along. What might seem like 3 miles may in fact be just 1 mile. Obviously, trekking times will vary from person to person, but in general, the times listed in this book reflect those of a moderate hiker — someone who will stop occasionally to take photos, eat some almonds and smell the proverbial roses.

DIFFICULTY

There are three trail ratings in this book: Easy, Moderate and Strenuous. The ratings are not scientific, but take into account the length of the trail, its terrain, the elevation change and the altitude. For example, a hike that's rated as Moderate at an elevation of 1,200 feet would be more challenging in the high country, and, therefore, could receive a rating of Strenuous. Also, in the same way that a chain is only as strong as its weakest link, the ratings often default to a segment of the trail. The Mescal Ridge Trail (see page 206) is a good example. Although the majority of that trail is easy, there's a stretch of about a mile that's moderate to strenuous. As a result, the trail gets an overall rating of Moderate. These variations will be detailed in the descriptive section of each listing. The bottom line: Know your limitations and abilities, and consult your physician before setting out.

Easy: Although it's never a good idea to go from the Barcalounger to the backcountry without some exercise in between, for the most part, if you're able to walk around the block a few times without needing supplemental oxygen, you should be able to handle the Easy hikes in this book.

Moderate: The Moderate hikes in this book require a healthy level of conditioning. If you do some kind of cardiovascular exercise at least three times per week, you should be OK. Also, if you're able to handle your local hikes — Camelback Mountain in Phoenix, for example — you'll be in good shape.

Strenuous: Unless you're an elite athlete, you shouldn't attempt a Strenuous hike without some serious training — jogging, running, elliptical, etc. These trails are generally long and steep, and they're not for the average hiker. Condition yourself by doing some Easy and Moderate hikes before graduating to the Strenuous class. Although it's never a good idea to hike alone, strenuous hikes in particular should always be done with someone else.

ELEVATION

The elevations listed for each hike refer to the highest points and the lowest points of the trail. On most trails in this book, those numbers coincide with the beginning and the ending of the hike, but not always. Also, keep in mind that elevation highs and lows are different than elevation gain. Because terrain tends to go up and down on most trails, you'll end up climbing more than the distance between the high point and the low point. The Oaks & Willows Trail (see page 122) is a good example. On that trail, the elevation ranges from 6,019 to 7,065 feet, for an elevation gain of 1,046 feet. However, the trail hits its highest elevation about halfway into the hike, and then drops down about 800 feet in elevation as it winds to the finish line. Those feet have to be made up on the way back out. So, instead of gaining 1,046 feet in elevation, you'll actually be climbing approximately 1,800 feet.

TRAILHEAD GPS

Although the accompanying maps for each listing will be enough to get you to the respective trailheads, we've also included GPS coordinates. However, the GPS coordinates are more likely to come into play if you get lost on the trail and need help finding your way back to the trailhead.

DIRECTIONS

Driving directions are included for each hike. Keep in mind that mileages are approximate, and that in some cases, roads might have more than one designation. For example, you might see a county road designation where you're expecting a forest road designation, or vice versa. Even though we've double-checked all directions, it's always important to call the appropriate governing agency — national forest, state park, etc. — before leaving home to get updates on detours, road closures and general conditions.

VEHICLE REQUIREMENTS
A few trailheads in this book can reached by paved roads, but most require some back-road travel on maintained forest roads. Some of these dirt roads are in better condition than others. The *Trail Guide* lists whether or not you'll need four-wheel-drive and/or a high-clearance vehicle. As a general rule, it's always best to have at least a high-clearance vehicle when venturing out into the wilds. During the winter and periods of heavy rainfall, some forest roads might be impassable or difficult to drive. And in higher elevations, such as the White Mountains, the roads might not be passable until May, depending on the winter snowfall and subsequent snowmelt. To avoid getting stranded and causing resource damage to these roads, wait until the road surface has hardened before venturing out. Call the ranger station or other governing agency for up-to-date information on road conditions.

DOGS ALLOWED
Most trails in Arizona allow dogs; however, some do not, including those in national parks. Where dogs are allowed, they must be on a leash and you must maintain control of your pet at all times. Also, keep in mind that pets could attract wildlife, including large carnivores.

USGS MAPS
The hikes in this book include maps with directions to their respective trailheads. Because all of the routes are well marked and relatively easy to follow once you hit the dirt, we didn't include detailed trail maps. However, ordering or downloading topographical maps from the U.S. Geological Survey website is strongly recommended. The *Trail Guide* identifies which map or maps you'll need, and getting them is easy. Simply visit www.usgs.gov/pubprod/maps.html, click the link to "download digital scans of topo maps," and then look for the "map locator" link. Once you have the maps, study them, learn as much as you can about the terrain, and then toss the maps in your backpack. You probably won't need them, but if you do, they can be a lifesaver. Plus, they won't add much weight to your pack.

INFORMATION
Rockslides, mudslides, fires, floods ... many things can affect access to the hikes in this book. Before you head out, it's important to check with the respective ranger stations or governing agencies for current trail information and road conditions — we list phone numbers and websites.

INTRODUCTION

BEFORE YOU GO

PHYSICAL CONDITIONING

Before you start lacing up your boots, you need to consider your own conditioning. Are you active? Inactive? With the exception of the Aspen Peak Trail (see page 82), nothing in this book is a walk in the park. These are rugged trails out in the wilderness, and choosing a hike that matches your level of conditioning is important. In other words, it's imperative that you know your body's limits. That said, you don't have to be an Olympic athlete to hit the trail. There's a hike inside for just about everyone.

Regardless of what kind of shape you're in, you'll need to learn some basic stretches and do them before venturing out. This helps avert injuries such as torn muscles. Keeping in good cardiovascular condition (with your physician's approval) through running, jogging or even steady walking — activities that raise your heart rate — will help you avoid gassing-out midway through a hike.

WHAT TO TAKE

Whether you're on a short desert hike or a 15-mile trek in the mountains, there are several things you should throw in your pack. Although some of this might seem like overkill, having the following provisions could turn a dangerous situation into an adventure you'll laugh about later.

Basic Equipment:

- Topographical map (sealed in a plastic bag)
- Pen and paper
- Whistle

- Waterproof matches
- First-aid kit (see page 15)
- Pocket knife or multitool
- Extra clothing (see below)
- Sunscreen
- Sunglasses
- Water (see page 15)
- Compass (a GPS device does not replace a compass)
- GPS device
- Fire starter or tinder kit
- Pocket flashlight (with spare batteries)
- Extra food (see below)
- Space blanket (lightweight emergency shelter)
- Insect repellent

Shoes and Clothing: What you put on your feet is arguably one of the most important decisions you'll make when preparing for a hike. It's best to consult with an expert at an outfitter such as REI or Cabela's or Babbitt's in Flagstaff, among others. They'll make sure you're looking at boots appropriate for day hikes, as opposed to boots for extended backpacking trips. They'll also make sure you have enough toe room, enough heel support, enough ankle support, etc. If your shoes are too tight, too loose or too uncomfortable, you'll end up being miserable on the trail, and you might injure yourself in the process. Another thing an outfitter can help you with is the "break-in" time for the various boots. They'll tell you what's necessary. Most boots won't require a lot of break-in time, but it's always a good idea to wear them around the house for at least a few days before using them on the trail.

What you wear on the rest of your body is important, too. The best advice is to layer up. It's easy and effective. Here's what you do. Rather than wearing one heavy set of garments, take several light layers of clothing that are easy to put on or take off as the weather and your body temperature change. Your minimum combination of layers should be comfortable during the warmer stages of your hike, while allowing you to add enough layers to stay warm when the temperatures drop.

Keep in mind that fabric choices can make a subtle, unexpected difference. On a windy day, a light windbreaker over a light wool sweater might actually keep you warmer than a heavy jacket that made you damp and sweaty earlier in the hike. Cotton won't insulate your body properly, especially if the weather is wet or cool or windy. Wool and synthetic fabrics do a much better job of keeping you warm. For desert hiking, it's best to wear cotton clothing, including a cotton hat. Although you might be tempted to wear shorts on desert hikes, long pants will do a better job of protecting you from cactuses and snakes.

Food: What you pack is a matter of taste. Just be sure to have a good combination of proteins and complex carbohydrates to keep your body energized for the entire hike. And without going overboard, pack more than you think you'll need. You'll burn a lot of calories out on the trail, especially on the hikes with Moderate and Strenuous ratings.

Water: A gallon a day is the general rule for water; however, if you're hiking the desert in the summer, which is strongly discouraged, you'll need at least double that amount. How much water you take depends on how much available drinking water is out there, and whether or not you're carrying a water-filtration system.

Because the hikes in this book are day hikes, it's feasible to carry as much water as you'll need in a Camelbak or some other hydration system. However, if you do get into a situation where you find it necessary to drink from a natural water source, be sure to filter it first. Even the purest-looking stream, spring or pool almost certainly harbors unwanted microbes — bacteria, viruses or parasites. Although they probably won't kill you, they can make you very sick. If you don't have a water-filtration system, you can use a closely woven fabric, such as a bandanna, to filter out mud and visible particles, but to guard against microorganisms, you'll need to boil the water or use chemical treatment (chlorine or iodine tablets).

Of course, portable water-filtration systems are the best option, and they come in many shapes and sizes. You won't have any trouble finding one that's easy to carry and easy to use. Consult with an expert at an outfitter before opening your wallet.

First Aid: What you carry depends on how much you know. As a general rule, you'll at least want to include Band-Aids, an antiseptic (iodine, Neosporin, etc.) for cleaning wounds and tweezers for removing splinters, cactus spines and dirt from cuts. A small comb can remove large cactus spines. Gauze and adhesive tape are also good to have, whether for tending to blisters or covering an open gash. You can easily carry many other items in a first-aid kit, but these are the basics. Most outfitters sell first-aid kits in varying sizes. Buying one is a good investment.

ON THE TRAIL

HIKING SOLO

Hiking alone can be very appealing; however, as a general rule, it's always better to hike with someone else. If that's not an option, make sure you have a good plan in place. Hiking solo is very different from hiking with others. It's more dangerous, but if you adjust your plan accordingly, you can minimize that danger. For example, take fewer risks by letting solitude be your adventure, rather than clambering over rockfalls or racing to the summit. If you can, get to know a region well before you go solo there. And even if you can't familiarize yourself in person, study the topo maps to learn about the terrain, and note the locations of roads and ranger stations. Also, memorize the major landmarks you'll be using to help pinpoint compass directions.

Of course, the most important thing is to make sure that someone knows where you're going — including which trailhead you plan to use if there are multiple starting points — and when you plan to return. Make it clear that if you're not back by a certain time, someone should call the authorities.

PHYSICAL MONITORING

When you're on the trail, you'll want to stay in tune with your body. Pay attention to little aches and pains, and don't ignore them. You'll also want to keep tabs on hydration. Thirst is a poor indicator of fluid requirements. If you're thirsty, chances are you're already dehydrated, so drink regularly and drink often. Your urine should be pale yellow, almost clear. If it starts to turn dark yellow, you need to stop hiking and drink some water. On the other hand, if your urine is clear all day, it means that you need to eat more. Hyponatremia is a dangerous condition that comes from ample water consumption, but not enough sodium, chloride and calcium consumption. Those elements help to keep the body's metabolism working. If you do suspect hyponatremia, find some shade, sit down and eat something.

The bottom line: Be smart. If you're not feeling well on the trail, stop. Think about what might be wrong. Don't just keep plodding on. If you're hiking with others, let them know what's going on. If you're too tired to keep going, ask your teammates to sit down and wait with you. If they want to keep hiking, tell them to sit down anyway and enjoy the views.

SAFETY

In many respects, the Arizona backcountry is less dangerous than a city freeway, but there are certainly things to watch out for. This book is not intended to be a comprehensive survival guide. Rather than trying to train you to expertly cope with every possible catastrophe, this guide offers that ounce of prevention — something you can use to make your wilderness experience safe and enjoyable. Here are the things you'll need to be most concerned about:

Flash Floods: Every year, flash floods kill dozens of people in Arizona. July, August and September are the most dangerous months. When you're out on the trail, look at the sky and know where you are. If you're in a canyon or a wash, think about where the drainage begins. If it begins 30 miles away, you might not see the storm sending a flood your way. If the canyon is only a mile long, a flood will come only if the storm is right on top of you. In long canyons where you might not see the storm, keep track of exits — places where you can climb to safety at a moment's notice. Being caught in even knee-deep water can be fatal, no matter how well you swim. When it's moving fast and full of debris, water can be extremely dangerous.

Keep in mind, the dangers go beyond the trail. Never drive across a wash or a dip in the road when water is flowing through it. Every year, people stall in as little as 2 feet of water. Then, when the water rises, it can carry the vehicle away, even if it's four-wheel-drive. Common sense will dictate most of these situations.

Lightning: Afternoon thunderstorms known as monsoons in Arizona often produce lightning strikes in desert regions and at higher elevations. These storms can develop quickly and move fast. Get a local weather report before you leave the house, and pay attention to the sky when you're out on the trail. During threatening weather, avoid lakes, meadows or open areas, exposed ridgelines, fence lines and peaks. Do not stand near large trees or other tall features. Avoid standing in wet areas. If caught in a lightning storm, assume a crouch position with your feet flat on the ground. If you're carrying a pack, put it on the ground below you and assume the crouch position on top of it. The pack will help insulate you from a strike.

Dehydration and Heatstroke: The sun in Arizona is powerful, so it's crucial to cover your skin, either with cotton garments and/or sunscreen. Shading your head with a hat or bandanna is important, too, and, if it's extremely hot, you should get them wet for an evaporative-cooling effect. Drink plenty of water the day before you hike so you don't begin your hike already slightly dehydrated. Of course, you already know that you need to carry plenty of water, but if you run out of water in the summer desert (why are you hiking in the desert in the summer?), rest in the shade until sunset and travel at night. If you must travel during the day, go from shady spot to shady spot or create your own shade with a blanket or tarp. Reduce water loss through your mouth by avoiding panting and talking. Limit eating — or don't eat at all — if your water is low or has already run out. In addition to carrying water on the trail, keep some in your vehicle so that you can rehydrate on the drive home.

Hypothermia: Also known as exposure, hypothermia is the lowering of the body's core temperature, and it isn't just a cold-weather concern. In fact, most cases of hypothermia occur in the summertime, when the temperatures are well above freezing — usually between 30 and 50 degrees Fahrenheit.

All it takes to get hypothermia is inadequate or damp clothing and a cool breeze. If that clothing gets wet, you go from dealing with a wind-chill factor to a wet-chill factor, which is even more dangerous. Your body temperature needs to drop only a degree or two to distinctly impair your judgment and reaction time. Add in fatigue, which plays a major role in robbing the body of warmth, and your judgment will be further compromised. You can't afford to be off your game in the wilderness.

If you're caught in rain or snow, or just get very damp, change into dry clothes with good insulation. Cotton, when wet, doesn't insulate. Choose wool or synthetic materials as base layers for most conditions. If only your feet are wet, switch to a pair of dry socks. Also, don't let yourself get chilled to the point of shivering, because that's already an early stage of hypothermia. Even a chilly wind can make your temperature drop if you aren't wearing a protective layer to hold your body heat in. Prevent hypothermia by staying dry and out of the wind, by wearing enough proper clothing, by keeping your head warm — 40 percent of your body heat is lost through your head — and by knowing the symptoms.

Symptoms of Hypothermia:

- Shivering (first warning sign)
- Fatigue
- Loss of coordination
- Incoherence, mumbling, stammering
- Hallucinations (advanced symptom)
- Pale appearance

- A warming sensation (can be a sign of very serious hypothermia; check other symptoms carefully)
- Goose bumps on skin
- Drowsiness

Altitude Sickness: The air is thinner — there's less oxygen — at higher elevations, which means you might feel differently than you do at lower elevations. Be alert to how your body responds to altitude change. Altitude sickness — also known as acute mountain sickness (AMS) — is most often developed beginning around 8,000 feet, and can affect anyone, regardless of fitness level. If you feel you're experiencing the symptoms of AMS, the best treatment is to stop and rest. While resting, breathe deeply and consume quick energy foods such as dried fruit, energy bars or candy bars. It's also important to stay hydrated. If your symptoms don't subside, head back down to a lower elevation, breathe deeply along the way and don't exert yourself any more than necessary. If symptoms continue to persist when you've reached a lower elevation, consider seeking medical attention.

Symptoms of Altitude Sickness:
- Headache, often severe
- Listlessness, drowsiness and fatigue
- Lightheaded feeling or dizziness
- Loss of appetite
- Nausea or vomiting

Rattlesnakes: Just to be clear, rattlesnakes aren't your main concern in the Arizona outdoors. Nevertheless, snakes are on the minds of a lot of hikers, so here's a little background.

As a general rule, rattlesnakes aren't very aggressive. Usually they'll rattle their tails to let you know they're around, and then slide off into the rocks or the grass to escape. The best place to find rattlesnakes is in thick ground vegetation — under, around and in large logs, and tucked into rock cracks. If you don't put your hands and feet into places you can't see, you probably won't be bitten by a snake or other poisonous reptile. In other words, when going over a large rock or log, don't step over the obstacle in one stride. Why? Your foot might wedge in near the base of the log or rock and disturb any crevice-lounging reptile. Instead, step up onto the log (or rock), then take a second step down on the other side, landing well clear of the base. Use a stick to bat the brush ahead of you before your feet get there. At night in the desert, snakes like to sprawl on warm, flat ground and on asphalt, so use a light.

Few people die from rattlesnake bites. Those most at risk are the extremely young, the extremely old and the allergic. However, it's still a painful injury. You've probably read about several ways to deal with venomous snakebites, with little agreement among doctors about which is best. If you do get bitten, stay as calm as possible. And sit still. Accelerated heartbeat from anxiety or exertion pumps the venom faster. If possible, get to a hospital quickly. Meantime, chemically activated cold packs, available at most drug stores, can slow down the venom's rate of travel. Apply the cold pack by wrapping it in a towel, shirt or bandanna so that it doesn't freeze your skin. If you must hike out on your own, set a moderate pace and remind yourself that this injury is not fatal. Try to stay calm.

If You Get Lost: Daniel Boone once said, "I ain't never been lost before, but I've been in some mighty strange country for three or four days." If you find yourself in a similar situation, sit down, stay calm and remember the acronym STOP (stop, think, observe and plan). People usually get lost because they panic. Instead, think back to when you last knew your location ... what have you done since? Backtrack to that spot. Look for landmarks. Use your map and compass, and don't second-guess your compass. Blow your whistle — other hikers might be in the area.

Because this book features only easy-to-follow day hikes, getting lost is unlikely. However, if you do get to that point, accept it and keep in mind that most hikers are found within 24 hours, especially if they've adhered to the cardinal rule of letting someone know where they planned to hike and when they planned to return. Meantime, find shelter, build a safe fire if necessary, and keep your energy up by snacking. One last thing: It's easier for rescuers to search you out when you're not running away from them, so stay put.

Wildlife: The backcountry is home to abundant wildlife. Species in Arizona include elk, mule deer, javelinas, black bears, mountain lions and even Mexican gray wolves. Although conflicts are generally rare, these animals can be dangerous if they're startled or if they sense you're a threat to their young or their food. If you're hiking with a partner, your conversation will usually create enough noise to prevent any surprise encounters.

If you do come face to face with a wild animal, remember: Keep children close at all times. Stay together in a group. Do not run. Running may trigger a chase instinct in some predators. Make noise to scare the animal or animals off. In the rare instance of being attacked by a predatory animal, fight back. If you're hiking with a dog, maintain control at all times and keep in mind that pets could attract wildlife, including large carnivores.

WILDERNESS ETHICS

For some reason, some people feel a need to leave their marks in the wilderness. The worst offenders like to carve their initials onto innocent aspen trees. Although leaving a mark might have seemed fitting a hundred years ago, when very few people ventured into these remote locations, it's an egregious crime today. It's bad for the trees, obviously. Plus, most hikers head into the wilderness to experience places unmarked by humans. That's why it's vital to adhere to the Leave No Trace principles.

Leave No Trace Principles

Plan Ahead and Prepare

- Know the regulations and special concerns for the area you will visit.
- Prepare for extreme weather, hazards and emergencies.
- Schedule your trip to avoid times of high use.
- Visit in small groups when possible. Consider splitting larger groups into smaller groups.

- Repackage food to minimize waste.
- Use a map and compass to eliminate the use of marking paint, cairns or flagging.

Travel and Camp on Durable Surfaces

- Durable surfaces include established trails and campsites, rock, gravel, dry grasses or snow.
- Protect riparian areas by camping at least 200 feet from lakes and streams.
- Good campsites are found, not made. Altering a site is not necessary.
- In popular areas:
    - Concentrate use on existing trails and campsites.
    - Walk single file in the middle of the trail, even when it's wet or muddy.
    - Keep campsites small. Focus activity in areas where there is no vegetation.
- In pristine areas:
    - Disperse use to prevent the creation of campsites and trails.
    - Avoid places where impacts are just beginning.

Dispose of Waste Properly

- Pack it in, pack it out. Thoroughly inspect your campsite and rest areas for trash or spilled foods. Pack out all trash, leftover food and litter.
- Deposit solid human waste in holes dug 6 to 8 inches deep at least 200 feet from water, camp and trails. Cover and disguise the hole when finished.
- Pack out toilet paper and personal hygiene products.
- To wash yourself or your dishes, carry water 200 feet away from streams or lakes and use small amounts of biodegradable soap. Scatter strained dishwater.

Leave What You Find

- Preserve the past. Examine, but do not touch, cultural or historic structures and artifacts.
- Leave rocks, plants and other natural objects as you find them.
- Avoid introducing or transporting nonnative species.
- Do not build structures or furniture or dig trenches.

Minimize Campfire Impacts

- Campfires can cause lasting impacts to the backcountry. Always use a lightweight stove for cooking and enjoy a candle lantern for light.
- Where fires are permitted, use established fire rings, fire pans or mound fires.
- Keep fires small. Only use sticks from the ground that can be broken by hand.
- Burn all wood and coals to ash, put out campfires completely and then scatter the cooled ashes.

Respect Wildlife

- Observe wildlife from a distance. Do not follow or approach animals.
- Never feed animals. Feeding wildlife damages their health, alters natural behaviors and exposes them to predators and other dangers.
- Protect wildlife and your food by storing rations and trash securely.
- Control pets at all times, or leave them at home.
- Avoid wildlife during sensitive times such as mating, nesting, raising young or winter.

Be Considerate of Other Visitors

- Respect other visitors and protect the quality of their experience.
- Be courteous. Yield to other users on the trail.
- Step to the downhill side of the trail when encountering horses and pack stock.
- Take breaks and camp away from trails and other visitors, when possible.
- Let nature's sounds prevail. Avoid loud voices and noises.

Source: Leave No Trace Center for Outdoor Ethics

WHEN YOU'RE DONE

The first thing you'll want to do when you've finished your hike is call your friends or family and let them know you've made it safely back to your vehicle. Obviously, you might not have cell service in some of the more remote areas, but call as soon as you can. After the hike, you'll also want to put on some dry clothes and drink some water. Even if you're not thirsty, there's a good chance you'll be a little dehydrated at the end of your hike. Finally, drive carefully, download your photos when you get home, share them with your friends and encourage them to follow in your footsteps. As John Muir once wrote: "Few are altogether deaf to the preaching of pine trees. Their sermons on the mountains go to our hearts; and if people in general could be got into the woods, even for once, to hear the trees speak for themselves, all difficulties in the way of forest preservation would vanish."

The Inner Basin Trail (see page 202) offers hikers an easy way to see fall color. | PAUL GILL

A full moon rises over West Clear Creek Trail (see page 64) near Camp Verde. | NICK BEREZENKO

WINTER

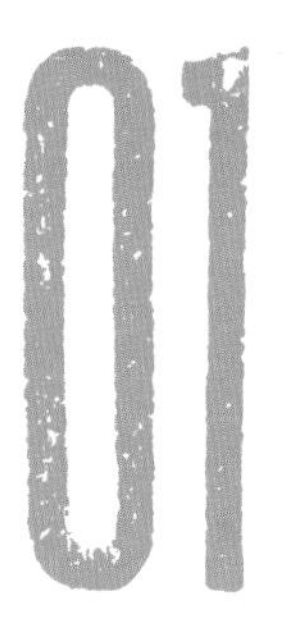

Badger Springs Trail

Agua Fria National Monument

There are a couple of things you should know about the Badger Springs Trail: 1) Badgers aren't among the mammals you're likely to see — your chances of seeing the trail's namesake are about as good as they are at Sun Devil Stadium. 2) Agua Fria, which is Spanish for "cold water," is the name of the river you'll be following, but the river is usually just a river*bed*, and it's almost never cold. Here's another thing: If you're a little squeamish about rattlesnakes, you might want to sit this one out — the desert sun stirs up Mohave greens and other rattlers as early as February.

Disclaimers notwithstanding, the Badger Springs Trail is one of Central Arizona's best, especially in the winter. Archaeology, ecology, history, spectacular scenery, peace and quiet are the selling points of this hike, which winds through the heart of Agua Fria National Monument, a 71,000-acre parcel of high mesa grassland 40 miles north of downtown Phoenix. Unlike other federal parklands, this one offers solitude — if the South Rim of the Grand Canyon is Grand Central, Agua Fria is a bus stop on a deserted stretch of Route 66.

Indeed, very few people have ever been to the monument. Millions, however, drive by it every year. The trailhead, which is within shouting distance of the Sunset Point Visitor Center, is located just off Interstate 17 at the

The usually dry Agua Fria River flows with spring runoff. | LES DAVID MANEVITZ

Waterfalls are a rare sight on the Agua Fria, except in winter and spring. | ELIAS BUTLER

Badger Springs Road exit. From the freeway, it's a short drive — less than a mile — down a forest road to the trailhead. That brings up another thing. Badger Springs Trail isn't really a trail. It's more of a route. From the "trailhead," you'll follow a traditional path for a few hundred yards down to the Badger Springs Wash toward the river. After that, the trail is whatever route you choose to take along the Agua Fria.

In the winter and spring, the river will be more substantial. Other times, it'll be nothing but a series of pools. Either way, what you'll quickly realize is that this hike is slow-going. That's because you'll be bushwhacking through a combination of soft sand (imagine walking on the beach in Santa Monica)

Richinbar Mine was named after one of the camp's most popular citizens, Richard M. Barker, and has several documented spelling variations, including Richen Bar, Richin Bar, Richenbar and, its most popular, Richinbar. Remains of the camp include a gravesite for miner Ed Barden, who had a heart attack when coming out of the mine in 1897.

and an endless stream of boulders, ranging in size from large pumpkins to Volkswagen Beetles. There's a lot of up and down and around and around on this hike, which makes it hard to gauge distance. Although the river runs for several miles to Black Canyon City, it's best to hike for an hour or two, and then retrace your steps.

Along the way, you'll experience one of Arizona's many beautiful riparian corridors. This one is home to cottonwoods, sycamores, willows, coyotes, bobcats, antelope, native fish and 177 bird species. The list goes on, but the monument wasn't established because of Mother Nature. It was created to protect more than 400 archaeological sites. From A.D. 1250 to 1450, a people known as the Perry Mesa Tradition inhabited this Precambrian canyon, and they left behind one of the most significant systems of prehistoric sites in the Southwest.

As you make your way downstream, keep your eyes peeled for their cliff dwellings and petroglyphs, as well as the old pipeline left over from the Richinbar Mine — interestingly, the rusted steel seems more like a museum piece than an eyesore. Of course, more than anything, you'll want to be on the lookout for snakes.

Petroglyphs are just some of the rewards for hikers along the Agua Fria riverbed. | LES DAVID MANEVITZ

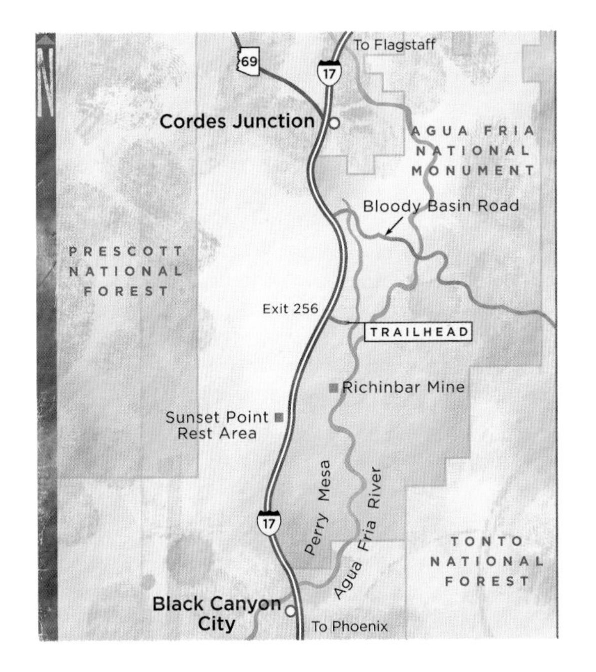

01 | TRAIL GUIDE

Length: Varies, depending on how far downstream you go
Difficulty: Moderate
Elevation: 3,122 (along the river) to 4,600 feet (in the monument's northern hills)
Trailhead GPS: N 34°13.878', W 112°05.996'
Directions: From Phoenix, take Interstate 17 north for approximately 40 miles to the Badger Springs Road exit (Exit 256) and turn right. Cross the gravel parking lot to Forest Road 9001 and continue for 0.75 miles to the trailhead.
Vehicle Requirements: None; accessible by all vehicles
Dogs Allowed: Yes (on a leash)
USGS Map: Joe's Hill
Information: Bureau of Land Management, 623-580-5500 or www.blm.gov/az

Bear Canyon Trail

Pusch Ridge Wilderness | Coronado National Forest

It's called Bear Canyon, and there *are* bears out there, but your chances of seeing a mountain lion are probably better. That wasn't always the case, but over the years, lions — also called cougars, pumas, catamounts and panthers — have mostly lost their fear of humans and now roam around in broad daylight, especially in this wilderness area. If you see one, maintain eye contact, make yourself look as large as possible, don't run, don't turn your back and never, ever say, "Heeere kitty, kitty, kitty." In most cases, the cat will hit the road and you can hit the trail, which begins at the Sabino Canyon Recreation Area visitors center.

From there, you have two choices: 1) take the shuttle bus to the Bear Canyon Overlook picnic area, or 2) start hiking immediately and skip the bus. Option No. 2 adds 3 miles overall to the hike, but they're easy miles and you won't be at the mercy of a bus schedule.

The longer route kicks off with a short walk on a wide dirt path known as the Bajada Trail. Don't be surprised if there are a lot of other hikers around you. This is a gorgeous park that attracts about 1.2 million people a year. Eventually, though, the crowds will thin out. That's especially true in the winter, when rain and melting snow make crossing Bear Creek a real challenge. In all, there are seven crossings en route to Seven Falls, which is the highlight of the hike. In fact, this route is often referred to as the Seven Falls Trail. Whatever it's called, when there's water in the creek, there aren't

Seven Falls, when they're flowing, are a unique sight on the Bear Canyon Trail. | JACK DYKINGA

A winter trek through Bear Canyon means wet feet are almost a certainty. | RANDY PRENTICE

many desert hikes that can compare to this one.

After about 15 minutes on the Bajada Trail, you'll see a sign for Bear Canyon. Head that way and enjoy the views. The saguaros, paloverdes, chollas, prickly pears, mesquites and more make this a classic Sonoran Desert landscape. Add in the horses you're likely to encounter and it becomes a scene from a John Wayne Western.

The trail winds through this movie set for about 45 minutes to the Bear Canyon Overlook bus stop. Just before you get there, take note of the gargantuan saguaros in the area — there are some real giants growing on the steep slopes. Equally impressive is the creek that begins just beyond the bus stop. It's the lifeblood of this riparian area, which is protected by the Pusch Ridge Wilderness Area.

Although the creek has a tendency to dry up at times, in the winter,

The Bear Canyon Trail is located within the Santa Catalina Mountains, which are known as *Babat Duag* ("Frog Mountain") to the Tohono O'odham, the native people of the area. In 1697, Father Eusebio Francisco Kino, who was in the region to establish missionaries, reportedly named the range for his sister, Santa Catarina. That spelling held for nearly 150 years before it was changed to Catalina.

you'll get a healthy dose of water. It's cold, and it's almost impossible to cross the creek without getting your feet wet. There are different strategies for getting to the other side. Some people take off their shoes, some people wear water socks and some people try rock-hopping. No matter, you will get wet, but it's a small price to pay for the grand finale. Plus, the sound of the trickling water is like Mozart — all portable electronic devices should be turned off and stowed away on this trail.

The trek along the creek will take about an hour, at which point you'll start climbing away from the water and come to a sign that reads: "No Shortcuts." This is the start of a long switchback that'll have you thinking you're backtracking and going the wrong way. You're not. It's one long switchback — one zig and one zag — that takes you a couple hundred feet up the side of the canyon. About 15 minutes later, the trail arrives at a signed intersection. The route to the right leads to Sabino Basin. The trail to the left leads 0.2 miles to the falls.

In all, there are seven falls, and collectively, they rank as one of the most unlikely sights on any trail in Arizona. Seeing a mountain lion or even a bear is one thing, but seeing a piece of Yosemite dropped into the Sonoran Desert is something else entirely. It's something special. As you'll see, those seven falls are definitely worth those seven soggy creek-crossings.

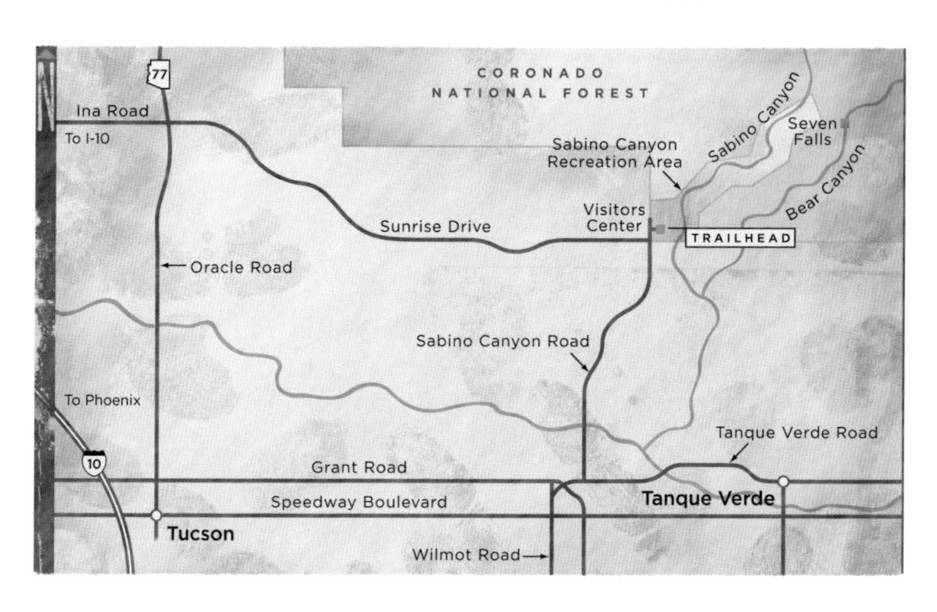

Length: 8.2 miles round-trip (from visitors center)
Difficulty: Easy
Elevation: 2,725 to 3,406 feet
Trailhead GPS: N 32°18.593', W 110°49.336'
Directions: From Tucson, take Tanque Verde Road to Sabino Canyon Road, turn left and continue 4 miles to the Sabino Canyon Recreation Area visitors center, which is open 8:30 a.m. to 4 p.m. daily.
Special Consideration: A $5 day pass is required.
Vehicle Requirements: None; accessible by all vehicles
Dogs Allowed: Yes (on a leash)
USGS Map: Sabino Canyon
Information: Santa Catalina Ranger District, 520-749-8700 or www.fs.fed.us/r3/coronado

Bog Springs/Kent Springs Loop

Mount Wrightson Wilderness | Madera Canyon

Elegant trogons are rare. In fact, Sasquatch has probably been spotted more often than the trogon, a colorful bird that migrates from Mexico to Madera Canyon in the spring. For bird-watchers in Arizona, the elegant trogon is the Holy Grail. It's related to the quetzal, and if you see one, consider yourself lucky. If you don't, don't worry. Your trip to Madera Canyon and the surrounding Mount Wrightson Wilderness Area won't be without reward. That's because this is one

Horsetail flourishes in the riparian environment of Bog Springs. | RANDY PRENTICE

About 200 species of birds inhabit the woodlands of the Bog Springs/Kent Springs Loop. | RANDY PRENTICE

of the most beautiful places in the Southwest.

In addition to the elegant trogon — and 199 other species of birds — the area is home to black bears, mountain lions, deer, coatimundis, coyotes, bubbling springs, green grasses, big trees and panoramic views. There are hiking trails, too, including the Bog Springs/Kent Springs Loop, which offers a quick and easy introduction to the area.

The trail begins in the Bog Springs Campground at site No. 13. The parking area, however, is located around the corner at the upper end of the campground. It's a short walk from one point to the other. From the trailhead, you'll follow an old road lined with yuccas and junipers for about 20 minutes to the intersection of the two trails. Bog Springs goes left; Kent Springs goes right. You can go either way, but you'll be happier going clockwise. Not because of the Coriolis effect, but because the Kent Springs Trail is steep in places, and you might prefer doing that section as a downhill, rather than as an uphill. It's up to you.

Artifacts of early Tohono O'odham tribes, including grinding holes known as *morteros*, can be found throughout Madera Canyon. Father Eusebio Francisco Kino, who was doing missionary work in the area, passed by the canyon in the late 1600s. Along with religion, his entourage brought cattle, which became the genesis of the region's large Mexican cattle ranches.

Veering left, the Bog Springs Trail follows a shallow basin cut into the western slopes of the Santa Rita Mountains. A forest of silverleaf oaks and ponderosa pines shades the trail as it meanders between springs sheltered by stands of gnarled Arizona sycamores. After about 40 minutes, you'll come to a second intersection with the Kent Springs Trail, which heads right. To the left is a short spur (0.1 miles) to Bog Springs. Before continuing the loop, head to the springs, where communities of moisture-loving plants cluster around the reliable water source, including Arizona bamboo, Arizona walnuts and colorful clumps of wildflowers. It's a nice diversion, and a great place to stop for a snack. Also, if you happen to have a Yorkiepoo in tow, it's an opportunity for man's best friend to get something to drink.

From Bog Springs, head back to the nearby intersection with the Kent Springs Trail and continue the loop. As you head southward, you'll climb gradually, with a few switchbacks thrown in. In all, you'll gain about 800 feet, and along the way the trees will open up from time to time, offering great views of Mount Wrightson and Madera Canyon. On clear days, the panoramas stretch westward to the Kitt Peak Observatory.

After another half-hour or so, you'll come to Kent Springs, which is the highest point on the hike and another great place to refuel. When you're ready to leave, don't be confused by the trail that continues uphill. Instead, take the Kent Springs Trail, which drops sharply to the right and follows an old jeep road that winds around to the trailhead. Heading back, if you're lucky, you'll see water running in the adjacent streambed. And if you're *really* lucky, you'll see an elegant trogon. But don't hold your breath. Your chances of seeing Sasquatch are probably better.

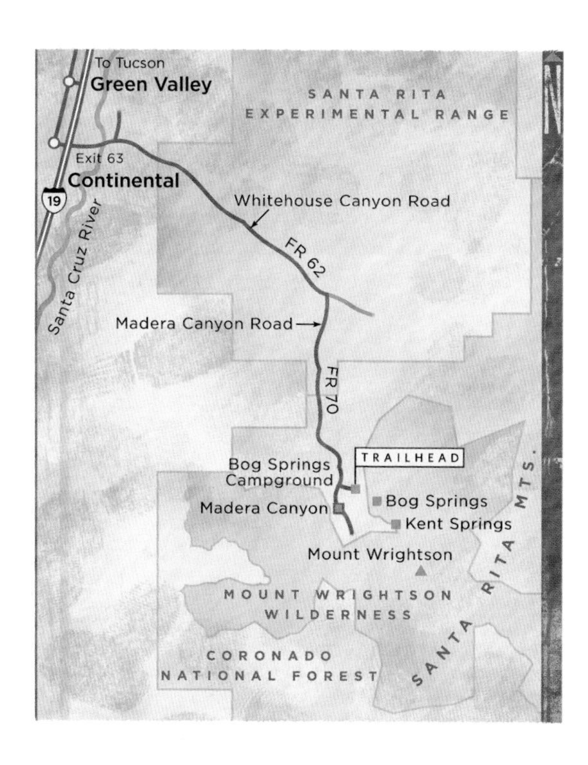

03 | TRAIL GUIDE

Length: 5 miles round-trip
Difficulty: Moderate
Elevation: 4,820 to 6,620 feet
Trailhead GPS: N 31°43.608', W 110°52.517'
Directions: From Tucson, drive south on Interstate 19 for 24 miles to Continental Road (Exit 63). Turn left and drive 1 mile to Whitehouse Canyon Road. From there, turn right and follow the signs for 5.6 miles to the Madera Canyon Recreation Area and the Bog Springs Campground. Turn left into the campground and drive around the loop to the trailhead.
Special Consideration: A $5 parking pass is required.
Vehicle Requirements: None; accessible by all vehicles
Dogs Allowed: Yes (on a leash)
USGS Map: Mount Wrightson
Information: Nogales Ranger District, 520-281-2296 or www.fs.fed.us/r3/coronado

Chillicut Trail

Four Peaks Wilderness | Tonto National Forest

Snow covers Brown's Peak near Phoenix in a winter view from the Chillicut Trail. | NICK BEREZENKO

Most people in metropolitan Phoenix, not just Sierra Club members, can point out the Four Peaks. It's the most prominent landmark looking east, and collectively, the peaks mark the highest point in the Mazatzal Range. Few people, however, have any idea what the individual peaks are named. And there's a reason for that: Three of the four summits *aren't* named. Brown's Peak, which is the highest (7,657 feet) and northernmost summit, is the only one with a name of its own. Fortunately, that won't affect your ability to enjoy this hike. The only thing that'll get between you and a perfect ending is the elevation gain of more than 3,700 feet. You'll earn bonus points for finishing this hike.

The journey — and that's the appropriate word — begins along Rock Creek on the east side of Four Peaks. For Phoenicians who have never seen the mountains from this perspective, the view alone is worth the drive, and it only gets better as the ascent unfolds. For the first few minutes, the trail is ill-defined while you work your way across the creek and up a short, rocky slope. Cairns are in place to help you along, and before you know it, you'll be on an old jeep road, marked as the Baldy Trail on USGS maps.

Sunrise and a storm collaborate over Brown's Peak. | NICK BEREZENKO

The Chillicut Trail follows the road for about 30 minutes, and it's all uphill. It's a concept you might as well get used to, because there's no real relief on this hike until you're headed back down, and by that time, your legs won't have any feeling left in them anyway. But don't let that discourage you. This is a great trail, and like so many others in this book, it doesn't get a lot of use, which means you'll probably have it all to yourself.

Where the jeep road ends, the trail veers left and cuts across one of the many small canyons you'll encounter before reaching Baldy Canyon, the main gorge on this trail. Although strenuous hikes require a certain determination and a plodding-on mentality, do yourself a favor and turn around from time to time. When you do, you'll get some great views of the Mogollon Rim to the north and Roosevelt Lake to the east. Moving on, about an hour into the hike, you'll come to a sign that instructs you to turn right for the Chillicut Trail. Most of this trail is easy to follow, but the sign is evidence that you're headed in the right direction. Things aren't so clear later on.

From the trail sign, you'll encounter a few creek-crossings and some ups and downs. The water, if there is any, won't be an issue, and the inclines and declines vary in length — kind of like having your StairMaster set on "random." The trail continues this way for about an hour, at which point you'll come to a set of very steep switchbacks that lead into Baldy Canyon. There's a creek in the canyon, and on the other side you'll see a sign announcing the Four Peaks Wilderness Area. This kicks off the best part of the trail.

In addition to the stream, the canyon features cottonwoods, willows, sycamores and the kind of lush vegetation that's typical of a riparian area. In particular, look for the young sycamores laying claim to the canyon. Someday, those sycamores will dominate, which is great news for hikers,

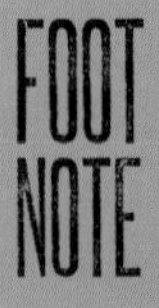

The Four Peaks are home to one of the country's premier amethyst mines — a private claim located at the end of a steep trail that produces some of the most brilliantly colored amethyst crystals in the world. According to some accounts, the Four Peaks lode was discovered in the 18th century by Spanish explorers. Although extensive mining began in the 1940s, mining activity ceased in the late '70s. Today, the claim-holders are digging around again. The area is protected by an electronic monitoring system and trespassing is prohibited.

because even in the winter, the shade from the trees is refreshing — at other times of the year, it can be a lifesaver. Beyond the shade, the trees provide habitat for the resident wildlife. Among the usual suspects are deer, skunks, javelinas, mountain lions and coyotes.

Heading up the canyon, the trail bridges the creek several more times and passes a primitive campsite that'll make you wish you had a sleeping bag on your back. Make a note of the location for some other time. From there, the canyon narrows, the underbrush gets thicker and the trail gets a little harder to follow. It also gets steeper, and more than once you'll equate the trail to the Energizer Bunny: *It just keeps going and going and going*. Eventually, though, you'll pass Chillicut Spring and arrive at an intersection with the Four Peaks Trail, which also marks the summit of Buckhorn Mountain.

If, by this time, your legs and lungs haven't already convinced you that you've made a long haul, the surrounding pine trees will. Their presence is what makes this hike unique. In a matter of miles, the Chillicut Trail goes from saguaros to ponderosas. It's a little mind-boggling, and it's a lot of work. Fortunately, it's all downhill from there. And better yet, for peak-baggers anyway, the summit has a name — something to write in a journal. That's not the case with three of the Four Peaks.

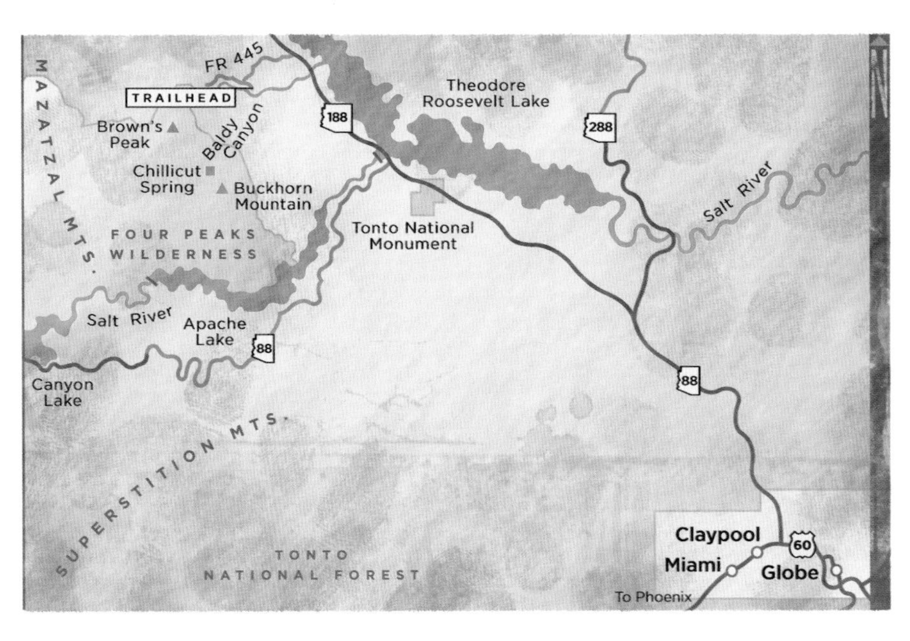

04 TRAIL GUIDE

Length: 11 miles round-trip
Difficulty: Strenuous
Elevation: 2,852 to 6,582 feet
Trailhead GPS: N 33°43.255', W 111°16.046'
Directions: From Claypool (near Globe), drive north on State Routes 88/188 for 36 miles to Forest Road 445 (Three Bar Road). Turn left onto FR 445 and drive 3 miles to Forest Road 445A. Turn left onto FR 445A and continue a quarter-mile to the trailhead.
Vehicle Requirements: High-clearance recommended
Dogs Allowed: Yes (on a leash)
USGS Map: Four Peaks
Information: Tonto Basin Ranger District, 928-467-3200 or www.fs.fed.us/r3/tonto

Echo Canyon Loop
Chiricahua National Monument

Walking in circles is usually discouraged, but not when it comes to hikes. Loop hikes are great because they're typically easy to follow and you never have to retrace your steps. Echo Canyon Loop is no exception. Like most loops, there's no right or wrong approach to this trail. In this case, most hikers opt for the counterclockwise route because it's a little easier. But really, there's nothing difficult about this trail, other than the challenge of coming up with enough adjectives to describe what is surely one of the most geologically unique trails in Arizona.

Whichever way you go, clockwise or counterclockwise, you'll have to navigate four trail junctions along the way. Although this is a loop, it's connected to most of the other trails in the Chiricahua National Monument, and as you'll see, it's easy to get distracted in this wonderland of lichen-covered hoodoos — the spectacular rock formations will have you looking this way and that.

From the trailhead, the counterclockwise route hits its first junction almost immediately. You'll see a sign that points toward the "Grottoes." Head that direction, but before you split, turn around and take a gander at the enormous rock formation in the distance known as Cochise Head. If you use your imagination, it looks as if the renowned Apache chief is lying on his back and looking up toward the sky. The nose and the forehead are prominent, and the natural feature that appears to be his eyelash is actu-

The Echo Canyon Loop trail is home to the mischievous-looking Dino Rock. | MOREY K. MILBRADT

Cochise Head is seen in repose from the Echo Canyon Loop trail. | LES DAVID MANEVITZ

ally a 100-foot-tall ponderosa pine.

Heading downhill, you'll arrive at the grottoes in a matter of minutes. Although these passageways invite exploration, it's important that you stay on the trail, not only because of the Leave No Trace principles (see page 19), but because there are several dangerous drop-offs within the grottoes. It's even more dangerous when it's wet, which is often the case in the winter, when snow and ice are common. The point is, stay on the trail. The Civilian Conservation Corps worked hard to build this route in the mid-1930s, and you need to stick to it.

Just beyond the grottoes is Echo Park, a lush cove dominated by Apache pines, Douglas firs and Arizona cypress. You shouldn't be tired at this point, but if the breathtaking beauty is taking a toll, this is a great place to kick back and take a break. In addition to the trees and the other greenery, there's an unexpected stream that runs through this little Eden in the winter and spring. There are even a few waterfalls that'll trick you into thinking you're somewhere else. Perhaps somewhere in North Carolina or maybe West Virginia.

The next segment of the loop heads into Rhyolite Canyon along the Hailstone Trail — again, pay attention to the nearby intersection and make sure you're headed toward the "Echo Canyon Parking Area." It's drier and

In 1887, shortly before she married fellow Swedish immigrant Neil Erickson, Emma Peterson bought a log cabin from a man named Ja Hu Stafford, and later transformed it into a ranch house, known as Faraway Ranch, which still stands today. After the couple's retirement, the ranch was once again transformed, serving as a dude ranch run by their daughter and son-in-law until the 1960s. Today, guided tours of the ranch are available.

hotter along this stretch, which skirts the south-facing wall of the canyon for just under a mile. After a mile, a third junction connects the Hailstone Trail to the Ed Riggs Trail. This is where the only workout on the route begins. This hike is rated as Moderate, and could almost earn an Easy rating, but along Ed Riggs there's an uphill climb that'll get your attention. It's nothing like the switches on the North Kaibab Trail (see page 210), but it's uphill all the way back to the trailhead. That, of course, completes the loop, however, if you have the time, you might want to make a detour at the loop's fourth intersection, which shows up about an hour-and-a-half into the hike.

The side trip leads to Massai Point, where the CCC built a wonderful lookout tower that offers views of most of the monument and beyond. In the distance, you can even see the Dragoon Mountains, which served as a stronghold for Cochise and Geronimo in their ongoing battles against the U.S. Army. Although the trek to Massai Point adds about a half-mile total to the Echo Canyon Loop, the views from the top are well worth the extra steps. Besides, on a trail where walking in circles is OK, there's certainly nothing wrong with getting sidetracked as well.

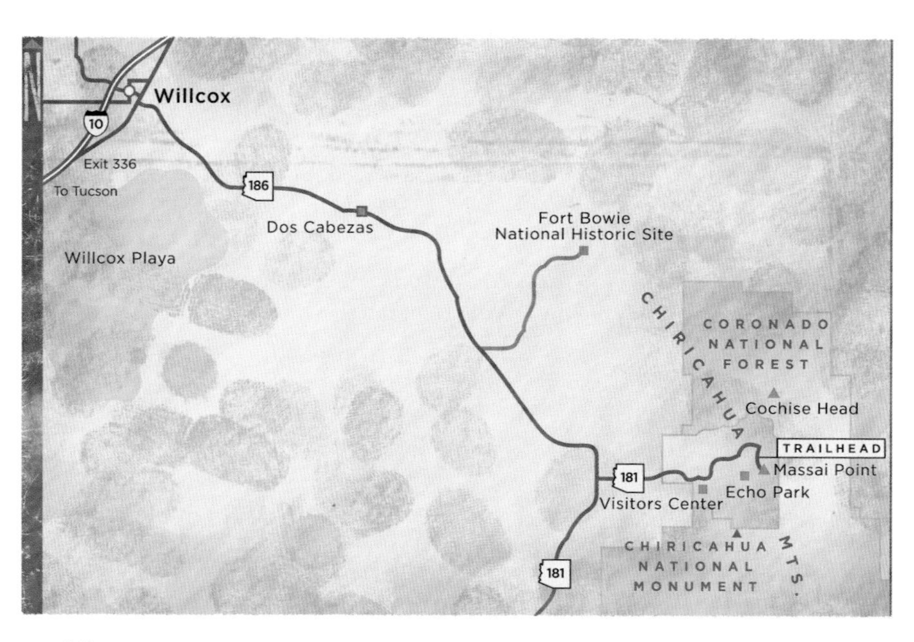

Length: 3.5 miles round-trip
Difficulty: Moderate
Elevation: 6,784 to 6,330 feet
Trailhead GPS: N 32°00.706', W 109°18.945'
Directions: From Tucson, take Interstate 10 east to the first Willcox exit. Veer right and drive 3 miles into town to the first stoplight. Turn right and follow State Route 186 for 32 miles to the junction of State Route 181. Turn left onto SR 181 and drive 4 miles to the Chiricahua National Monument entrance. The trailhead is located at the Echo Canyon Trail Parking Area, 5.5 miles past the visitors center on Bonita Canyon Drive.
Special Consideration: National Park Service fees apply.
Vehicle Requirements: None; accessible by all vehicles
Dogs Allowed: No
USGS Map: Cochise Head
Information: Chiricahua National Monument, 520-824-3560 or www.nps.gov/chir

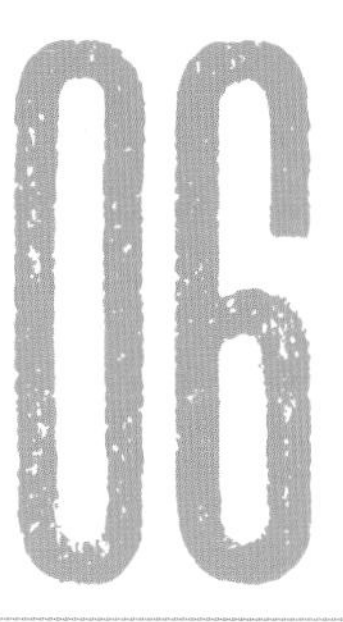

Hamburg Trail

Ramsey Canyon Preserve | Coronado National Forest

Don't let the name fool you. This trail has nothing to do with sauerkraut, strudel or Sergeant Schultz. The name comes from Henry Hamburg, a prospector from St. Louis who developed a mining camp at the head of Ramsey Canyon. Adding to the confusion is the fact that most people refer to this hike as the Ramsey Canyon Trail. Nomenclature notwithstanding, this is one of the most scenic and diverse hikes in Arizona, and even though it appears in the Winter section of this book, it's a great option all year long. Fall is exceptionally beautiful.

Before you get started, you'll have to obtain a permit from The Nature Conservancy's visitors center — the first part of the hike crosses their preserve. The fee is minimal, and it's well worth the expense, especially if you appreciate wildlife.

In particular, Ramsey Canyon Preserve is considered one of the best bird-watching sites in the world. In the winter, if you know what you're looking for, there's a good chance of seeing dark-eyed juncos, yellow-rumped warblers, red-naped sapsuckers and ruby-crowned

Snow lightly dusts the ground in Ramsey Canyon. | PAUL GILL

A hiker is nearly indiscernible next to a sycamore tree in Ramsey Canyon. | DAVE BLY

kinglets. And even if you can't tell one of those birds from a pterodactyl, there's something appealing about knowing that they're out there. The same goes for the Coues white-tailed deer, which wander in and out of the creek without any apparent fear. No doubt they've been conditioned by the benign nature of the resident bird-watchers. Nonetheless, in January, the bucks are in their rut, so avoid wearing any musky perfumes.

The Miller Peak Wilderness Area, which was established in 1984 and encompasses 20,190 acres, is located in the Huachuca Mountains of Southeastern Arizona. Huachuca is an Apache word that means "thunder." It most likely refers to the high volume of thunder and lightning that occurs in the area during the summer monsoons.

The trail begins at the back door (literally) of the visitors center, and the first thing you'll see is Ramsey Creek, a key tributary of the San Pedro River. About 10 minutes later you'll come to the James Cabin. It was built in 1902, and as you stand there looking around, you'll agree that few cabins in the history of westward expansion could have had a better view. It's impressive, and so is the Arizona sycamore nearby. It might not be the oldest tree in the canyon, but it dates back to 1760, which makes it old. Very old. Even older than Cochise, by a long shot.

From the big tree, the trail moves uphill and includes some minor switchbacks before crossing into the Coronado National Forest and the Miller Peak Wilderness. Your reward for climbing this far is a good overlook of lower Ramsey Canyon and the San Pedro River Valley. Above the switchbacks, the trail drops back down to the creek and follows it through a riparian zone as lush and beautiful as any you'll find in the Southwest. Imagine having Oak Creek Canyon all to yourself. It's that remarkable.

Along this stretch, small waterfalls tumble past gnarly sycamores and lacy-limbed firs, and the trail crosses the creek five or six times as it climbs toward the upper elevations of the Huachuca Mountains. Eventually, after an hour-and-a-half and 2.5 miles, you'll come to a point where the Hamburg Trail intersects the Wisconsin Trail, which leads into Wisconsin Canyon. This is the turnaround point for this listing, but before you head back, make a perimeter check. Along with the scenic beauty, this area includes the remains of some leveled homesites that were part of Henry Hamburg's mining camp. There's not much left, but the area makes a great place to stretch your legs and grab a snack. Strudel would be good if you have it.

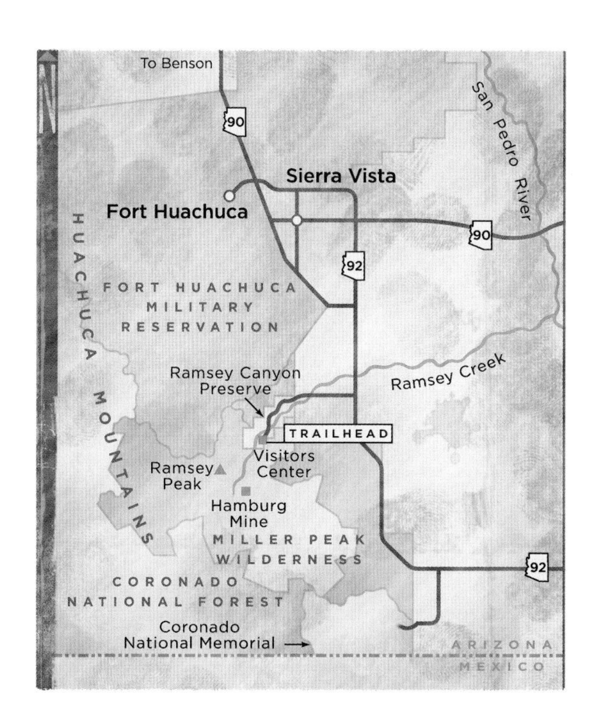

06 | TRAIL GUIDE

Length: 5.6 miles round-trip
Difficulty: Moderate
Elevation: 5,498 to 6,826 feet
Trailhead GPS: N 31°26.860', W 110°18.443'
Directions: From Sierra Vista, drive 6 miles south on State Route 92 to Ramsey Canyon Road and turn right. Follow Ramsey Canyon Road for 3.5 miles to The Nature Conservancy's Ramsey Canyon Preserve parking area and trailhead.
Special Consideration: Because the preserve is on private property, a permit is required to hike across it to the Hamburg trailhead. The preserve is open from 8 a.m. to 5 p.m.
Vehicle Requirements: None; accessible by all vehicles
Dogs Allowed: Yes (on a leash)
USGS Map: Miller Peak
Information: The Nature Conservancy, 520-378-0311 or www.nature.org/arizona

Loy Canyon Trail

Red Rock/Secret Mountain Wilderness | Sedona

Of all the hikes in the Sedona backcountry, Loy Canyon Trail is one of the best. First, it's never too crowded, which is wonderful, but hard to understand. Second, Steller's jays are everywhere. When you catch a glimpse of blueprint-blue out of the corner of your eye, it's a jay — the contrast of the blue birds against the red rocks is striking. More colorful than Matisse. And then, of course, there's the trail itself, which is why you're reading this book in the first place.

The trail begins at the mouth of Loy Canyon, which is surrounded by the picturesque beauty you think of when you think of Sedona. For the most part, there's no sign of civilization, other than the Hancock Ranch, which you'll see to the left within the first 15 minutes of the hike. After that, it's all Mother Nature, with a mix of scrub oaks, Arizona cypress, yuccas and prickly pear cactuses at the lower elevations and alligator junipers, ponderosa pines, Gambel oaks and firs at the higher elevations. The transition becomes obvious after about 20 minutes, which is when you'll come to an enormous ponderosa pine. It won't be the last, but it's one of the first.

From there, the wide well-constructed and easy-to-follow path winds along a usually dry creekbed. You'll be climbing gradually, but you'll hardly notice. What you will notice is the pair of rock formations that dominate the skyline. To the left is Loy Butte and to the right is Secret Mountain. On this hike, you'll be headed toward the latter. But first, you'll be tested by a

The views from Secret Mountain include Sedona's iconic landscape. | LARRY LINDAHL

The Loy Canyon Trail leads hikers to a pine forest. | NICK BEREZENKO

The nearby Palatki and Honanki cliff dwellings are thought to have been occupied between A.D. 1100 to 1300 by the Southern Sinaguan people, and some of the earliest pictographs within the dwellings date back to the Archaic period, between 3,000 and 8,000 years ago, before the dwellings were even created.

series of switchbacks. They begin about 4 miles into the hike, and they'll get your attention. In all, you'll gain more than 1,000 feet in the next mile — to get to the top, you have to run this gauntlet. Not only is it steep, but the incline has been seized in places by unforgiving undergrowth. It's prickly and unwelcoming. Complicating things further are the remnant pieces of fencing wire, which may have been left by the Samuel Loy family, who used this 5-mile trail in the 1880s to run cattle to and from the summer pastures on the rim.

Eventually, after what feels like a lot of bushwhacking, you'll come to a saddle that connects Secret Mountain to the Mogollon Rim. This is where the Loy Canyon Trail intersects the Secret Mountain Trail. At this point, you'll have hiked about 2.5 hours, and you could turn around. Instead, you should veer right and continue about 200 yards to the top of Secret Mountain.

The landscape is mostly flat and shady, and it's a perfect place for a nap or a picnic or a first kiss. If none of that appeals to you, you could add some distance to the overall hike by continuing less than a mile southward to the old Secret Mountain Cabin. Or what's left of it, anyway. Turns out, the surrounding ponderosa grove is more impressive. And that's typical. Like everything in the Sedona backcountry, the man-made stuff takes a backseat to Mother Nature.

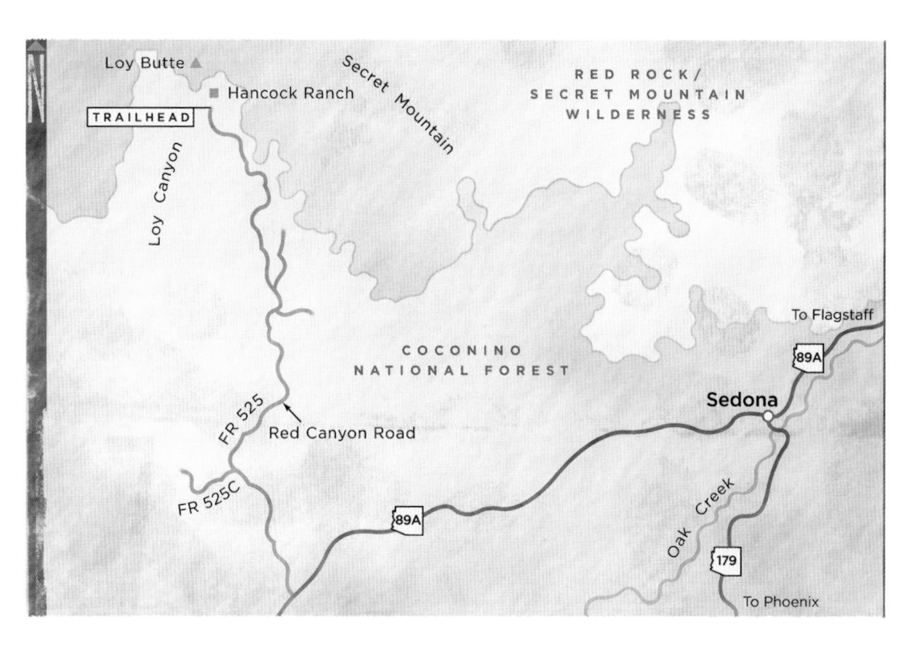

Length: 10 miles round-trip
Difficulty: Moderate
Elevation: 4,679 to 6,400 feet
Trailhead GPS: N 34°55.943', W 111°55.479'
Directions: From the roundabout junction of State Route 179 and State Route 89A in Sedona, drive south on SR 89A for 9.7 miles to Forest Road 525. Turn right onto FR 525 and continue 9.5 miles to the trailhead.
Special Consideration: A $5 Red Rock parking pass is required.
Vehicle Requirements: None; accessible by all vehicles
Dogs Allowed: Yes (on a leash)
USGS Map: Loy Butte
Information: Red Rock Ranger District, 928-282-4119 or www.fs.fed.us/r3/coconino

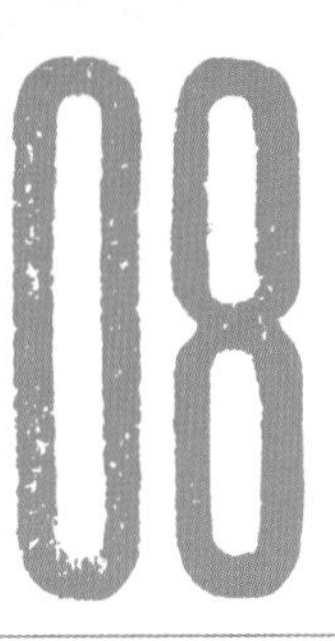

Pine Mountain Trail

Pine Mountain Wilderness | Prescott National Forest

If you think the Road to Hana is a long and winding road, take away the pavement, throw in a creek-crossing, long stretches of washboard effect and a lifetime supply of deep ruts, and you've got the road to Pine Mountain. Unlike most of the hikes in this book, this one is tough to get to, but the scenery and the solitude on the trail are well worth any car sickness you might acquire along the way. Plus, the drive itself is beautiful — it's the 5-10 mph, enforced by the infrastructure, not the sheriff's department, that'll catch up with you.

The Pine Mountain Trail, as this listing is called, is actually a series of four trails that lead up to and around Pine Mountain, which rises 6,814 feet above the wilderness of the same name. The route begins at the Salt Flat Trailhead, where a handful of dispersed campsites scream out: "Sleep here, man. You've already endured the long and winding road, you might as well stick around and make the most of it." If you've got the time, it's good advice. As campsites go, this one certainly measures up. And so does the nearby hike.

The first of the four trails is the Nelson Trail, which takes you into the Pine Mountain Wilderness, an isolated area that was established in 1972 and encompasses 19,569 acres. On a map, it's not all that far from the Red Rock/Secret Mountain Wilderness near Sedona, but in terms of usage, it's halfway around the world. The lack of foot traffic is something you'll appreciate as you make your way through the shaded riparian area fed by

A small pool takes on a wintry look in the Pine Mountain Wilderness. | ELIAS BUTLER

Arizona sycamores are common along the Pine Mountain Trail. | TOM BEAN

Sycamore Creek. This stretch is a wonderland of trees dominated by Arizona sycamores, ponderosas and alligator junipers. Appreciate the combo. Seeing this trio of trees grouped so closely together is rare, but on this trail, it's a way of life.

After about 15 minutes, the trail arrives at the remains of the old Nelson place, an abandoned homestead that includes a series of impressive stone walls. If you've ever been to Virginia, you can envision what it looks like. The Nelsons, of course, are no longer there, but if they were, you'd want to tip your hat as you go by and congratulate them on being smart enough to homestead this tract of land. In your head, you'll be thinking: *This is the kind of scene Robert Frost would have written about. How was anybody lucky enough to live here?*

From the Nelson place, the trail winds along Sycamore Creek, crossing back and forth, for about 20 minutes until it reaches an intersection with the Pine Flat Trail, which veers right into Beehouse Canyon. Don't let the name fool you. This isn't your turn. Instead, continue following the creek upstream for another 45 minutes to a junction with the Willow Springs Trail. You'll be on that trail later in the hike, but for now, stay right on the Nelson Trail and look around. In addition to the inherent beauty and quiet

The road to the Pine Mountain Wilderness runs through Dugas, which is named for Fred Dugas, who established a ranch there in 1879. He considered his place the geographical center of Arizona. Legend has it that he cared so much about his cattle that he kept track of where they liked to lie down, and subsequently planted trees in those places to give them some shade. With more settlers entering the area, the need for a post office arose and, as was customary, one was established in the Dugas ranch house.

splendor that's typical of most wilderness areas, this part of the trail is marked by waves of young 10-foot ponderosas that are reclaiming the land after a fire burned the west side of Pine Mountain in 1989.

Literally, you'll be rubbing elbows with these lime-green trees as you make your way uphill to the Cloverleaf Junction, where the Nelson Trail meets the Pine Mountain Trail. This is the second of the four trails, and it angles left along Bishop Creek for about 45 minutes to an intersection with the Verde Rim Trail, about a half-mile southwest of Pine Mountain. Before you get there, you'll see more remnants of the fire, and you might see some snow as well, depending on what kind of winter it's been. Although this is considered a year-round hike, you should call the Forest Service ahead of time to check on the conditions.

At the Pine Mountain-Verde Rim intersection, turn left and continue northeast. As the name implies, the Verde Rim Trail hugs a narrow ridge that even mountain goats might appreciate. What the name doesn't tell you is that the views from the ridge are superb and include panoramas of Humphreys Peak, the Verde River Canyon, the Mazatzal Mountains and even Horseshoe Lake near Phoenix.

Moving north, just beyond a short side trail that leads to the summit of Pine Mountain, the Verde Rim Trail descends a series of steep switchbacks that lead to a saddle at the head of Sycamore Creek. Turn left onto the Willow Springs Trail, the fourth of the four trails, and follow it for a half-hour to its intersection with the Nelson Trail, and then another hour back to the Salt Flat Trailhead. In all, the route winds up and down for almost 10 miles. It's rated as Moderate, but it'll seem easy compared to the long and winding drive back to civilization. Not to worry, though. It's a beautiful drive.

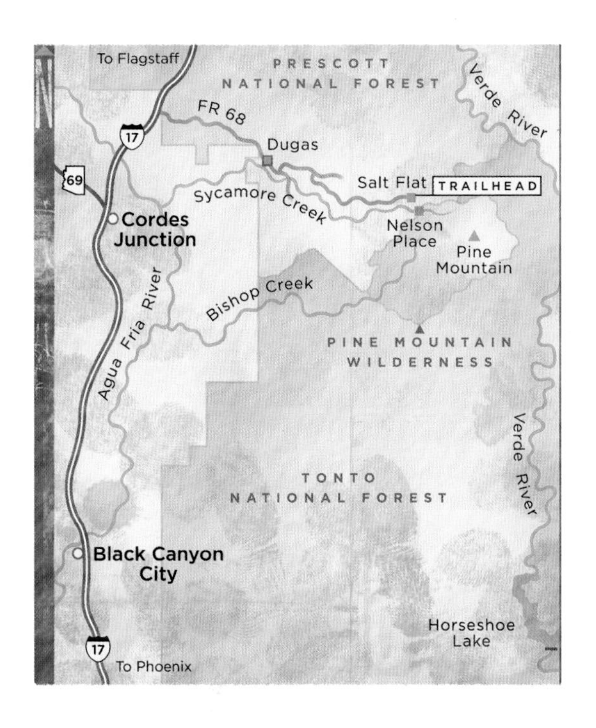

08 | TRAIL GUIDE

Length: 9.6 miles round-trip
Difficulty: Moderate
Elevation: 5,110 to 6,814 feet
Trailhead GPS: N 34°19.577', W 111°50.177'
Directions: From Phoenix, drive north on Interstate 17 for 57 miles to the Dugas Road exit. From there, take Forest Road 68 southeast for 18 miles to the trailhead for the Nelson Trail at the boundary of the Pine Mountain Wilderness.
Vehicle Requirements: High-clearance vehicle required
Dogs Allowed: Yes (on a leash)
USGS Map: Tule Mesa
Information: Verde Ranger District, 928-567-4121 or www.fs.fed.us/r3/prescott

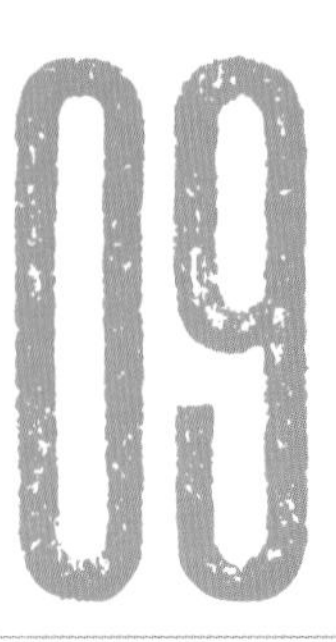

Pioneer Trail

Pinal Mountains | Tonto National Forest

The Pinal Mountains are not in Spain. Or Central America. Or Argentina. They're about an hour's drive from Phoenix, and not much farther from Tucson. That said, they might as well be on another planet. Ask hikers in either of those cities about their favorite trail in the Pinals, and most will look at you as if you'd just asked to

Hikers are treated to some spectacular panoramic views on the Pioneer Trail. | NICK BEREZENKO

A grove of manzanitas grows along the Pioneer Trail. | NICK BEREZENKO

borrow their deodorant. There's a universal "huh?" when you talk about this quiet mountain range near Globe. For whatever reason, people rarely venture into it, and that doesn't make any sense. For several reasons.

There's the convenient proximity to civilization, of course, but more importantly, there's the solitude and the scenic beauty. The Pinal Mountains are among the state's handful of sky islands — high-elevation zones surrounded by desert — which means a 95-degree day among the saguaros in Phoenix can easily become a 65-degree adventure among the ponderosas of the Pinals. Geographically, it's not all that different from a trek in the White Mountains or the Santa Catalinas.

The high point of the Pinals is Pinal Peak, which tops out at around 7,800 feet. This is where most of the trails are headed, and there are several to choose from: Icehouse, Bobtail, Telephone. The best introduc-

Legend has it that Ike and Phineas "Finn" Clanton and other members of the Clanton Gang retreated to the Globe area shortly after the infamous shootout between the Earps and the McLaurys at the O.K. Corral in Tombstone in 1881. Historians later argued that Phineas wasn't involved in the shootout; however, he did live in Globe after the gunfight, and when he died, he was buried in the Globe Cemetery. His grave is still there today.

tion to the area, however, is along the Pioneer Trail. It's rated as Moderate, and the trailhead is located just south of the Pioneer Pass Recreation Area, which, like the mountain range itself, is another hidden gem. Built by the Civilian Conservation Corps in the 1930s, the rec area is a perfect place for a family picnic or a post-hike hootenanny.

Getting back to the hike, one of the first things you'll notice is that the sign for the trail reads: Squaw Springs Trail. For obvious reasons, the name has been changed, but the signs have not. Nevertheless, it's the same trail, and it kicks off with a series of switchbacks that cut through a forest of stately ponderosas and Flintstone boulders. After about 15 minutes, look to the right for a sensational panorama to the northeast. A few minutes later, you'll come to a grove of manzanitas that rivals any grove on any hike in Arizona. As you'll see, the trail serves as a tunnel through the thicket. It's almost primeval.

From there, the route continues its uphill climb — in and out of the forest — to a long series of well-built steps that lead to even more rocks and trees, including maples. Beyond this point, the trail is overrun at times by thorny bushes that seem to laugh at hikers who attempt the trail in shorts — do yourself a favor and wear long pants. Eventually, after an hour or so, you'll arrive at a place where the trail is blocked by a fallen ponderosa. The route is a little tricky to find at this point, but if you look 90 degrees to the left of the log, you'll see where to go.

A few hundred feet later, you'll pass through a cattle gate and come to a forest road, which services the surrounding radio towers. To the right is a cluster of boulders, some of which are bigger than a bread truck. Walk that way and check out the rocks. The views from their tops are out of this world. You can't quite see Phoenix, but rest assured, it's not very far away.

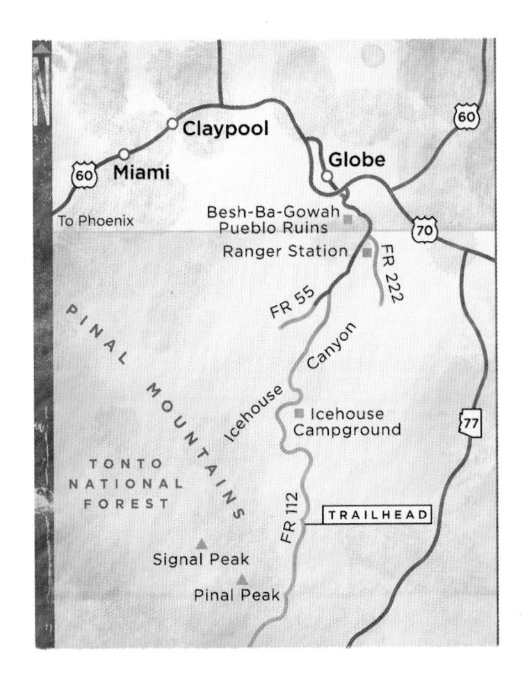

09 | TRAIL GUIDE

Length: 4.6 miles round-trip
Difficulty: Moderate
Elevation: 6,156 to 7,800 feet
Trailhead GPS: N 33°16.152', W 110°48.178'
Directions: From Globe, follow the signs toward Besh-Ba-Gowah Pueblo Ruins. Just past the turnoff, turn right onto Icehouse Canyon Road and continue 1.7 miles to the intersection of Forest Road 112 and Forest Road 55. Veer left onto FR 112 and continue 6.9 miles to the Pioneer Pass Recreation Area. The trailhead is another 1.5 miles to the south.
Vehicle Requirements: None; accessible by all vehicles
Dogs Allowed: Yes (on a leash)
USGS Map: Pinal Peak
Information: Globe Ranger District, 928-402-6200 or www.fs.fed.us/r3/tonto

Summit Trail

Camelback Mountain | Phoenix

It's true; climbing Camelback can be frustrating. The parking is a nightmare, too many hikers wear too much perfume, and the single-file line can feel like the queue at a Jimmy Buffett concert. If you go on a weekday, though, especially late morning or early afternoon, things are usually different. You'll never experience the solitude of Old Baldy (see page 214) or the Widforss Trail (see page 176), but at least you won't be dealing with the weekend onslaught of imprudent "trailgaters," a fitting and self-explanatory term coined by former *Arizona Highways* intern Leah Duran, our favorite hippie chick.

Weekend or weekday, onslaught or off-day, this trail is a must. It leads to the highest point in metro Phoenix. It's an iconic landmark that can be seen from the window seats of approaching 747s. And it's one of the capital city's points of pride. It's also a great workout that'll have even the best-conditioned hikers huffing and puffing by the end. It's only 1.2 miles to the top, but in that short distance it climbs more than 1,200 feet. Factor in the sunshine and the thermometer, and it'll make anybody work up a sweat.

Like a lot of mountains, there's more than one way to the top of Camelback. In this case, there are two: 1) the Cholla Trail, which approaches from the east, and 2) the Summit Trail (a.k.a. the Echo Canyon Trail), which approaches from the west. The latter is the most popular, and if you're going up only once, this is the route to take.

It begins at Echo Canyon Park, which has very limited parking, especially on weekends, when the wait for a space can last up to an hour. From the trailhead, the hike immediately begins an uphill climb that won't let up until you're on your way back down. After a

Birds and helicopters get the best views of Phoenix's Camelback Mountain. | JEFF KIDA

The Summit Trail is popular with hikers and dog-lovers alike. | JEFF KIDA

series of long steps, the trail winds around an enormous boulder, about the size of a Dairy Queen, which is used by novice rock-climbers as a training site. About 15 minutes later, you'll come to a small saddle that offers great views of Paradise Valley below and the Praying Monk rock formation above. The Monk is a well-known local landmark and another popular hangout for rock-climbers.

From the saddle, the trail continues southward to another series of steps, which are followed by a set of handrails that help guide hikers up a steep series of boulders. This stretch tends to get clogged with hikers slowly making their way. Be patient, be careful and be respectful of others. There's a final set of handrails before the trail tops out on the nape of the camel's neck and winds to a narrow gully. From this point forward, there's not an actual trail. You simply make your way over and around the many boulders that dominate the terrain all the way to the summit.

At the crown of the gully, views to the south open up — you can see

During the late 1800s, the federal government set aside Camelback Mountain as an Indian reservation. By the 1940s, however, most of the mountain fell into private hands. Efforts by county, state and federal officials to restrict development above the 1,600-foot level were met with little success. Then, in 1965, the Preservation of Camelback Mountain Foundation, which was led by Barry Goldwater, spearheaded community efforts to save as much of the summit as possible. Those efforts ultimately led to a land exchange in 1968. President Lyndon Johnson and Secretary of Interior Stewart Udall attended the official ceremony.

downtown Phoenix and beyond. This is a good place to catch your breath and gear up for the hike's most strenuous stretch, which is another field of boulders, similar to what you'll have conquered in the gully. This gauntlet, however, is much longer and much more difficult. Not only will you be trying to catch your breath, you'll be dodging the downhill hikers who are gingerly skipping from rock to rock, just hoping to maintain their footing. In terms of balance, going up is easier than coming down, but you won't appreciate that while you're trudging up and gasping for breath.

Eventually, you'll come to another saddle, the third in all. Although your mind will trick you into thinking you're at the top, you're not. This is what's known as Camelback's false peak. Say a few choice words if you must, but keep on trekking. The true summit is just a few minutes away. When you reach the peak, you'll be surrounded by exasperated hikers — because the summit is relatively flat and comfortably wide, people tend to hang out up there for a while, catching their breath, eating energy bars and taking in the 360-degree panorama. If you look in their faces, you'll see that most of the hikers are feeling a sense of accomplishment, and justifiably so. After enduring the parking, the perfume and the trailgating, they've certainly earned it.

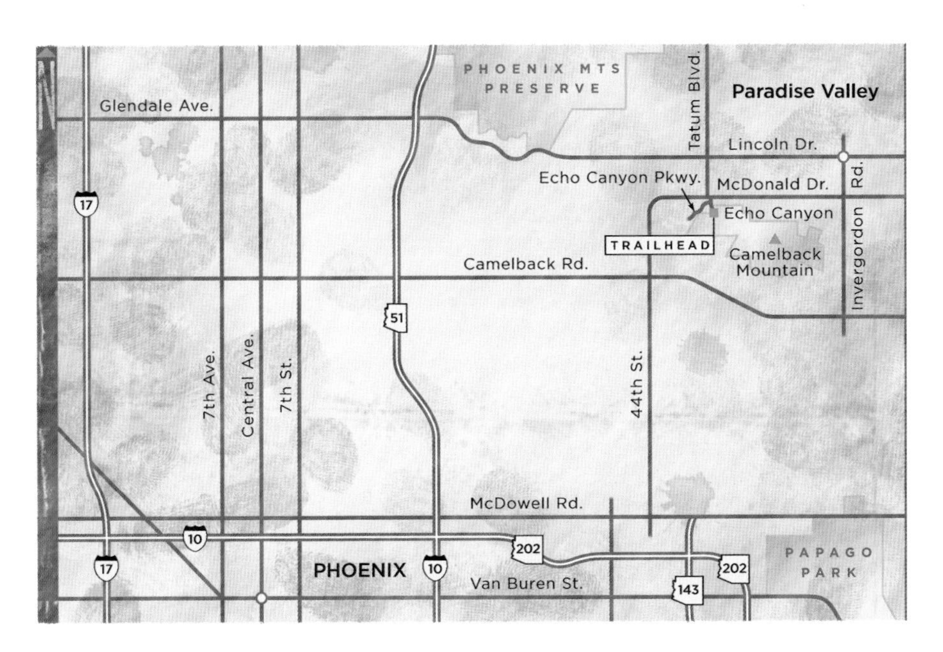

Length: 2.4 miles round-trip
Difficulty: Moderate
Elevation: 1,476 to 2,704 feet
Trailhead GPS: N 33°31.287', W 111°58.417'
Directions: From Phoenix, drive north on 44th Street to its intersection with Tatum Boulevard and McDonald Drive. Go right on McDonald Drive for one block and turn right onto Echo Canyon Parkway, which leads to the trailhead parking. The parking area is open sunrise to sunset, and parking is extremely limited.
Vehicle Requirements: None; accessible by all vehicles
Dogs Allowed: Yes (on a leash)
USGS Map: Paradise Valley
Information: City of Phoenix, 602-262-6862 or www.phoenix.gov/parks/hikecmlb.html

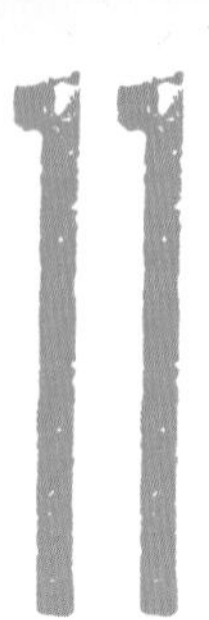

West Clear Creek Trail

West Clear Creek Wilderness | Verde Valley

The centerpiece of this hike, and the body of water for which it was named, is West Clear Creek, an idyllic stream that winds for nearly 40 miles through some of the most scenic and least-visited terrain in Arizona. And it's true — the creek itself is very clear, but, ironically, some of the directions you may have seen for the trail are not.

An older version of Forest Service directions, for example, suggested starting the hike at Clear Creek Campground. Technically, that's not wrong. In the same way you could start the hike in Flagstaff and traipse down Interstate 17 to the creek, you could also kick off this trek at the campground, but you'd have to do a lot of bushwhacking, and you don't want to do that. Instead, begin at Bull Pen Ranch at the end of Forest Road 215.

Not only will this plan spare you a lot of cuts and bruises, the scenic drive to the old ranch is an added bonus. Although FR 215 is a little rough in places, if you go slowly, a sturdy sedan will do. Of course, high-clearance is always the best option on back roads in Arizona. Either way, the road offers terrific views of the canyon into which you'll be hiking — as you look down, your Lewis and Clark impulses will shift into overdrive.

From the trailhead, the route passes under a canopy of impressive sycamores — you'll also see cottonwoods, Arizona walnuts, willows and ash along the creek. Initially, the trail piggybacks an old ranch road on the north bank of the creek. Then, after about a mile, it cuts south for the first

West Clear Creek winds for nearly 40 miles through Central Arizona. | DEREK VON BRIESEN

of four stream-crossings. Throughout most of the year, other than the wet season, it's a simple hop, skip and jump to the other side. In fact, if you're even mildly agile — you don't have to be one of the Flying Wallendas — you can maneuver over the rocks and logs without getting wet. Be careful, though, anything you step on will be slippery.

Heading east on the south side of the perennial creek, the trail meanders through a lush riparian forest and quickly comes to the second creek-crossing, followed by the official boundary of the wilderness area. Looking around, you'll understand why Congress designated more than 15,000 acres as the West Clear Creek Wilderness in 1984. From the soaring cliffs of Coconino sandstone to the hanging gardens of maidenhair fern and other vegetation, West Clear Creek is a natural wonder that attracts not only humans, but also bears, deer, mountain lions, badgers and birds galore. Be on the lookout.

Eventually, after 5.5 miles and a fourth creek-crossing, you'll come to a point where the trail veers northward from the creek. This is our recommended turnaround point. Just retrace your steps. If, however, you're in excellent condition and you want to extend the hike, follow the trail north through a draw that climbs 1,800 feet in 2 miles. It's strenuous all the way to a trailhead on Forest Road 214A. From there, it's possible to return to your car by following FR 214A for 1.3 miles to the upper end of the 2.5-mile Blodgett Trail, which completes a 15-mile loop. Whichever route you choose, in the end, you'll be glad you started at Bull Pen Ranch — that extra bushwhacking would have gotten you off on the wrong foot.

FOOT NOTE

Hundreds of years ago, the West Clear Creek drainage was also home to the Sinaguan people, who left behind ruins, tools and other artifacts that are now scattered throughout the wilderness area. If you're lucky enough to stumble upon such a treasure, enjoy it with your eyes only — do not touch it, move it or remove it. Leave it as it is for the next lucky explorer.

Late-afternoon sunlight warms a tree-lined bank along West Clear Creek. | DEREK VON BRIESEN

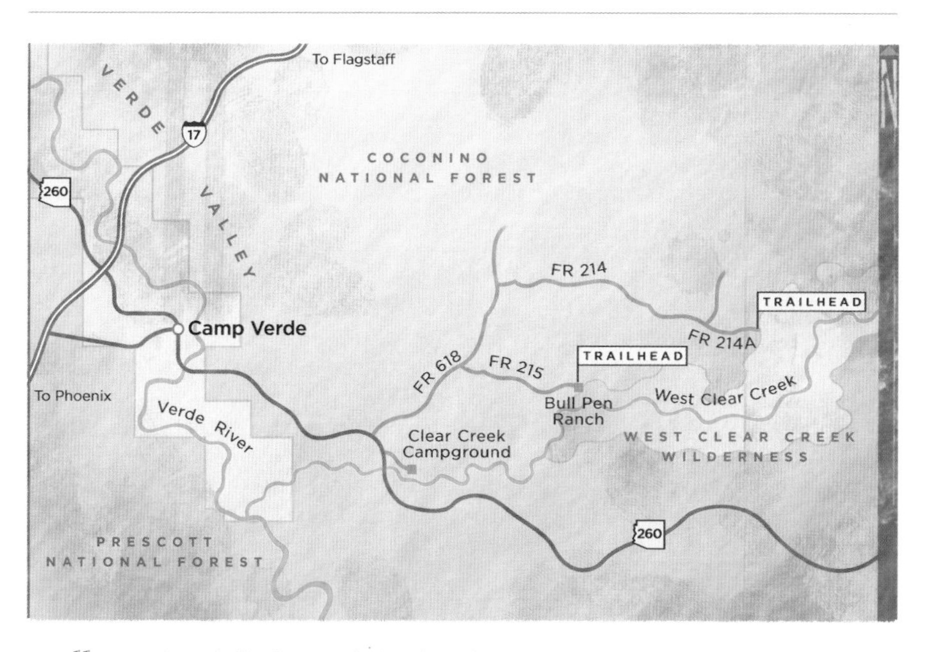

Length: 11 miles round-trip (along the creek only)
Difficulty: Easy (strenuous if you complete the loop)
Elevation: 3,700 to 4,100 feet (along the creek only)
Trailhead GPS: N 34˚32.338', W 111˚41.510'
Directions: From Camp Verde, drive southeast on State Route 260 for 6 miles to Forest Road 618. Turn left onto FR 618 and drive 2.2 miles to Forest Road 215. Turn right onto FR 215 and continue approximately 3 miles to the Bull Pen Ranch Trailhead.
Vehicle Requirements: High-clearance recommended
Dogs Allowed: Yes (on a leash)
USGS Maps: Walker Mountain, Buckhorn Mountain
Information: Red Rock Ranger District, 928-282-4119 or www.fs.fed.us/r3/coconino

West Fork Oak Creek Trail

Red Rock/Secret Mountain Wilderness | Sedona

If you're looking for isolation, this hike won't deliver. On weekends and holidays, especially in the spring and the fall, literally hundreds of people will be in your way. However, in the same way you don't avoid the Grand Canyon just because 5 million people a year visit the park, you don't want to leave the West Fork of Oak Creek off of your to-do list. In fact, if you have an absolute aversion to hiking with the masses, a good option is to skip the busy season altogether and take this hike in the winter. Admittedly, fall is best because of the autumn color, and spring is great because of the high water, but winter in Oak Creek Canyon can be magical, too, provided there isn't too much snow or ice. Use your head, and check with the ranger station before hitting the trail.

Regardless of when you go, there are several reasons this is the most popular trail in the Coconino National Forest: the towering cliffs of Coconino sandstone, the Douglas firs and box elders and bigtooth maples, the perennial stream, the wild grapes and asters and lupines, the mule deer and Abert's squirrels, and the list goes on. Those are just some of the reasons the federal government designated the canyon's first 6 miles, which includes this trail, a Research Natural Area in 1931. The ecosystem is extraordinary, which is why people from around the world flock to this trail.

The hike begins at the Call of the Canyon parking area, which is conveniently located just off State Route 89A in Oak Creek Canyon. In addition to West Fork, the fee area also serves as a starting point for the

Weather permitting, winter is a great time to hike the West Fork Trail. | DEREK VON BRIESEN

The West Fork Oak Creek Trail is the most popular hike in the Coconino National Forest. | DEREK VON BRIESEN

Thomas Point Trail and the Call of the Canyon Nature Trail. In fact, you'll be taking the nature trail for a half-mile out to the trailhead for West Fork. When you get there, you'll notice the ruins of an old settlement, including a root cellar of sorts cut into one of the nearby rock walls. If this were private property today, you couldn't put a price on it. Fortunately, it's public, and it's the last set of man-made structures you'll see.

Although the West Fork Trail is rated as Easy, it does include several creek-crossings that require a little agility and a willingness to get your feet wet — that's something to keep in mind if you're hiking in the winter. There are stepping stones or logs in most places, but there are no guarantees of keeping dry. The first of the many crossings occurs within a few minutes after leaving the trailhead. After that, they show up regularly. As alluring as the water is, it's the iconic red rocks that'll take your breath

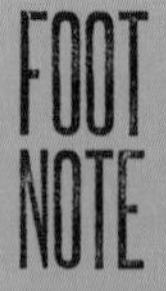

A few hundred yards past the footbridge that leads to the West Fork Trail you'll pass an old settlement that includes remnants of fireplaces, stone floors and a cliff house. They're leftovers from the Mayhew Lodge, an early 20th century dwelling. The homestead is believed to have been the inspiration for Zane Grey's book *Call of the Canyon*. In its heyday, the lodge was a favorite getaway of movie stars, politicians and writers, including Lord Halifax, President Herbert Hoover, Clark Gable, Susan Hayward, Cesar Romero, Jimmy Stewart and Walt Disney.

away. Hiking this trail is akin to walking in Manhattan for the first time. You'll be craning your neck a lot. Mesmerized. Spellbound. Captivated. Later on, when you're looking through your photos, you'll notice that most of them were taken with the camera pointed upward. That's just how it is.

The route continues along this same basic path — water, woods and natural wonder — for about 45 minutes, at which point the trail veers 90 degrees to the left. As you make your way through the canyon, you'll notice some alternate paths from time to time. It can be mildly confusing, but if you choose the trail closest to the creek, you'll be OK.

A few minutes after the sharp turn, you'll come to an area where a rockfall occurred, and just beyond that the canyon opens up a little. To this point, the trail has been well-marked and easy to follow. Beyond this point, the canyon is narrower and overgrown with vegetation. Most people turn around in this area, but if you're feeling adventurous, the next mile is worth the minimal bushwhacking.

The homestretch begins amid a pile of dead trees that have washed down from upstream. The trail is hard to find, but if you look to your left you'll see where it climbs up the canyon wall and away from the water before dropping back down again about 10 minutes later. At the 4-mile mark, which takes about 2 hours to reach, a decent-sized pool marks the end of the trail. This is the turnaround point for this listing; however, you might run into some backpackers who will keep on trekking. For them, the creek continues for 14 miles to the other end of the canyon. For everyone else, it's time to turn back, put up with the people and enjoy one of Arizona's very best hikes. You won't be the only hiker on the trail, but it won't matter. This trail is that good.

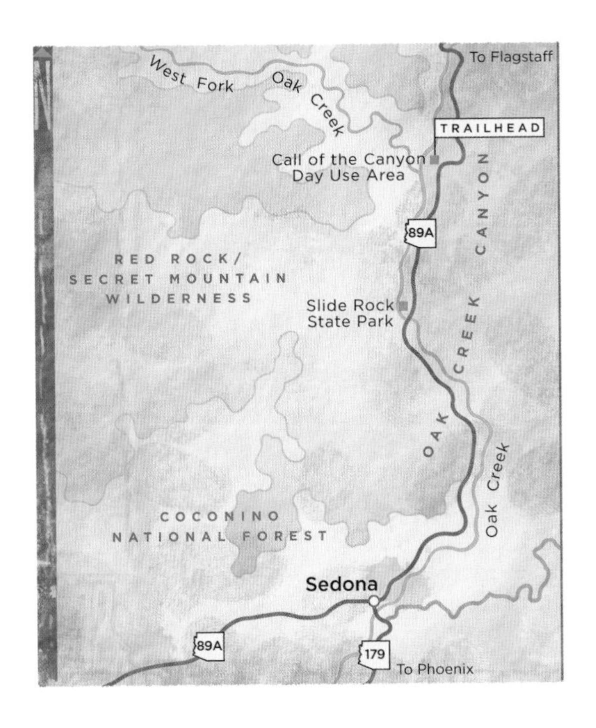

12 | TRAIL GUIDE

Length: 8 miles round-trip
Difficulty: Easy
Elevation: 5,328 to 5,619 feet
Trailhead GPS: N 34°59.434', W 111°44.587'
Directions: From Sedona, drive north on State Route 89A for 9.5 miles to the Call of the Canyon parking area.
Special Consideration: The Forest Service requires a $5 parking permit along the highway and a $10 per vehicle (up to five people) fee in the Call of the Canyon parking area.
Vehicle Requirements: None; accessible by all vehicles
Dogs Allowed: Yes (on a leash)
USGS Maps: Dutton Hill, Mountainaire, Wilson Mountain, Munds Park
Information: Red Rock Ranger District, 928-282-4119 or www.fs.fed.us/r3/coconino

Woods Canyon Trail

Munds Mountain Wilderness | Sedona

Unless you're a Tarahumara Indian, extreme trail running is usually ill-advised. Unlike the reclusive super athletes of Mexico's Copper Canyons — men and women who have the ability to run for hundreds of miles at a time — the average hiker is in no condition to tackle rugged terrain at breakneck speeds. With the proper training, maybe, but otherwise, you'd be better off blasting your kneecaps with a Louisville Slugger. The end result would be about the same. Of course, there are always exceptions, and the one trail that might be doable at a faster pace is the Woods Canyon Trail near Sedona, which is a favorite among local residents.

This well-graded and easy-to-follow trail begins at the south end of the ranger station parking lot on State Route 179. After a few minutes, you'll come to a log that serves as a connecting point to the other side of Dry Beaver Creek, which may or may not have water in it. Despite the moisture level of the creek, the landscape will likely include Herefords, whose orange-red hides match the red dirt of the initial stretch of trail. A few minutes later, you'll come to a gate, beyond which is an old jeep road. By the time you've closed the gate, the sounds of State Route 179 will have disappeared and the striking mesas ahead will be grabbing your attention, along with the wide open trail — Tarahumara or not, it's on this stretch that you'll really feel like running.

About 20 minutes later (less time if you decide to run), after having

The Woods Canyon Trail follows Dry Beaver Creek and is a favorite among Sedona residents. | KIM HOSHAL

Dry Beaver Creek gets its distinctive red color from the area's soil. | KIM HOSHAL

crossed a few small washes, you'll come to a trail register and a larger wash that's home to some beautiful Arizona sycamores and other riparian species. Beyond the big wash, the trail is more shaded. It's not shady, but it's shadier, which doesn't matter much in the winter, but makes a big difference in the summer. Deer like the tree cover, too. You'll see plenty of hoof prints as you make your way along the creek and into Woods Canyon. As always, use plenty of caution when entering wash areas, especially on cloudy days. Rain can be lovely in an open meadow, but it can be deadly in the desert.

Moving along, the trail hugs the wash for a few hundred yards before passing through a cattle gate and a barbed-wire fence. Up ahead you'll see an intersection. The Horse Mesa and Hot Loop trails go left, and the Woods Canyon Trail veers to the right. Five minutes later you'll cross into

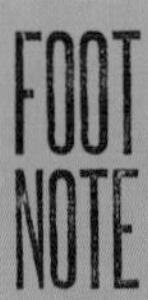

The Munds Mountain Wilderness and its highest peak are named for pioneer rancher James T. Munds. In 1883, he homesteaded a clearing northeast of the mountain, known as Munds Park, from which he ran cattle to winter pastures in the Verde Valley. Today, the top of Munds Mountain has one of the most spectacular and underappreciated views in the entire Red Rock area.

the Munds Mountain Wilderness Area and catch your first glimpse of red rocks. Unlike some of the more famous trails to the north, this trail isn't dominated by the picturesque geology that epitomizes Sedona. Instead, the highlight is a beautiful riparian area and plenty of solitude. There's not a lot of traffic on this route, but there's no good reason for that. It's a gorgeous trail, especially after about an hour, when the ponderosas and the hardwoods start showing up.

As beautiful as the trees are, the best part of the trail actually begins about a quarter-mile farther, where Rattlesnake Canyon merges with Woods Canyon. At this point, the trail dips into the enormous, boulder-strewn wash of Dry Beaver Creek. Your best photos of the day will be taken from atop one of the Frigidaire-sized rocks in this area. Although the scenery is spectacular, keeping tabs on the trail can be a little tricky. Stay left along the wash and you'll see the trail within a few minutes.

The rest of the route climbs gradually for about 20 minutes and eventually gets to a point where the hike's most prominent red rocks come into view. They're not as striking as Cathedral Rock or any of the other nearby landmarks, but they do make a magnificent centerpiece in a landscape that doesn't really need one. The rocks mark the end of this hike. At this point, you'll have trekked a little more than 4 miles, with 4 more to go on the way back. For the average hiker, that's a decent day hike. However, if you're feeling adventurous and you have plenty of time, you can extend the hike by boulder-hopping through Woods Canyon all the way to Interstate 17. Although it's not as challenging as running for hundreds of miles in the Copper Canyons of Mexico, it will elevate your stature beyond that of an average hiker. Be careful, though. You're not a Tarahumara.

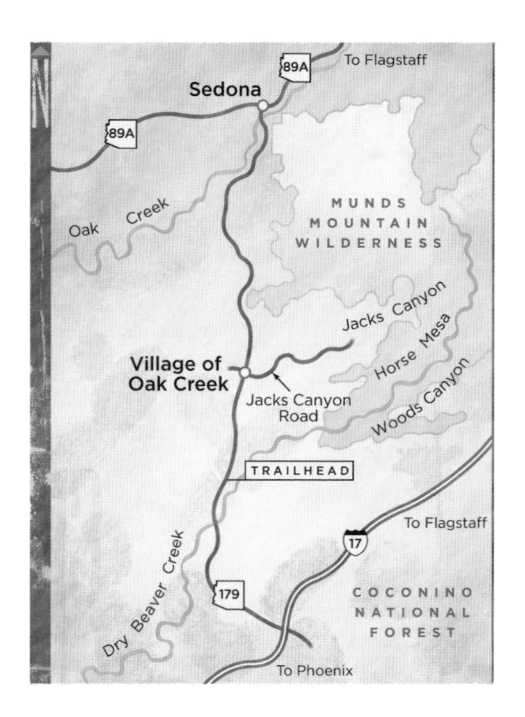

13 | TRAIL GUIDE

Length: 8.5 miles round-trip
Difficulty: Easy
Elevation: 3,905 to 4,165 feet
Trailhead GPS: N 34°45.371', W 111°45.793'
Directions: From Sedona, drive south on State Route 179 for approximately 8.5 miles to the Sedona Ranger Station. The trailhead is at the south end of the parking lot.
Vehicle Requirements: None; accessible by all vehicles
Dogs Allowed: Yes (on a leash)
USGS Maps: Munds Mountain, Sedona
Information: Red Rock Ranger District, 928-282-4119 or www.fs.fed.us/r3/coconino

Oak Creek highlights many trails in Sedona, including Casner Canyon (see page 78). | DEREK VON BRIESEN

SPRING

Allen's Bend/Casner Canyon Trails

Coconino National Forest | Sedona

Although it can lead to trouble, some of the most spectacular trails in Arizona are surprisingly accessible. The Bright Angel Trail (see page 94) on the South Rim of the Grand Canyon is probably the best example. Think about it, there's nothing — no long drive on a primitive road, no technical requirements, no checkpoint for unqualified hikers — to keep the hordes from venturing into a place that requires much more than an afterthought: "Hey, as long as we're here, let's grab a Diet Coke and hike down to the river. Everyone's doing it. Let's go." Unfortunately, the number of ill-equipped visitors who tackle the Canyon instead of ordering a sandwich at El Tovar, where they'd be out of harm's way, is too high. And maybe that's why Mother Nature put a moat around the Casner Canyon Trail.

There's no way around it. If you want to hike this scenic trail, you'll first have to wade through the waist-high waters of Oak Creek. Although the water levels will fluctuate throughout the year, you're definitely going to get wet, especially in the spring — unlike the West Fork Oak Creek Trail (see page 68), where the creek-crossings can be done with a few simple rock-hops, there aren't any natural bridges in this vicinity to facilitate your needs. But don't let that deter you, unless, of course, you'd feel more comfortable having lunch at El Tovar.

Although there's only one

Hikers in Casner Canyon get uninterrupted views of Sedona's famous red-rock formations. | DEREK VON BRIESEN

To get to Casner Canyon, hikers must first cross Oak Creek. | DEREK VON BRIESEN

way to reach Casner Canyon itself, there are two ways to access the trail of the same name. The first is to park on the narrow shoulder of State Route 89A (a Red Rock parking pass is required), and then follow a steep path down the embankment to the trailhead. This is not your best option. Instead, park at Grasshopper Point, where a Red Rock parking pass is required, and hop on the Allen's Bend Trail. It's a short and beautiful connector trail that winds for a half-mile along Oak Creek to its intersection with the Casner Canyon Trail. That's all there is to Allen's Bend. Alone, it won't satisfy avid hikers. However, it's ideal for anyone who wants a dose of Sedona's natural environment, but isn't conditioned for backcountry hiking.

From the intersection of the trails, turn right onto the Casner Canyon Trail, cross a normally dry creekbed and make your way to the banks of Oak Creek. There's no magic formula for getting across. Shoes on, shoes off, it doesn't really matter. Either way, you'll want to be careful. The rocks below the surface will be extremely slippery. If you have a walking stick, this is the time to use it. Also, be sure to secure any electronic gear (cameras, GPS devices, iPods) in a waterproof bag. It's not unusual for even graceful hikers to fall victim to the unscrupulous nature of the slippery

Carl Schnebly, who arrived at Oak Creek in 1900, used what is now known as Schnebly Hill Road to transport lumber from Flagstaff to build a two-story, 11-room home that's now the site of the Los Abrigados Resort. Once his home was completed, Schnebly used the road, which offers scenic views of Casner Canyon, to transport wagonloads of produce north to Flagstaff and supplies south to his small general store. He also petitioned for a post office, which he proposed calling either "Oak Creek Crossing" or "Schnebly Station." Both names were rejected because they were too long to fit on a cancellation stamp. So he named the new postal site after his wife, Sedona.

rocks. Be prepared and aim for the cairns on the opposite bank.

Once you're across, hug the rock ledge and follow the trail into Casner Canyon, which is small compared to Munds Canyon to the north, but enormous when it comes to payoff — the red-rock views from this trail are breathtaking, and can't be seen from a backseat window. About 20 minutes into the hike, you'll notice a large Utah juniper, the most common cedar in Arizona. You'll also notice the quiet. At this point, you'll be separated from the car noise of Sedona, and, more than likely, you'll be alone. This trail doesn't get the kind of traffic that other hikes in Sedona get, which makes the panoramic views even that much better.

Not far from the big juniper, the trail begins its gradual climb up from the canyon floor. It follows the north side of the canyon and quickly loses the shade of the riparian habitat below. Even in the springtime, the heat will take its toll, so carry plenty of water and go heavy on the sunscreen. Moving along, the gorgeous scene in front of you will command your attention, as it should, but make sure you turn around every once in a while and look the other way. All of the views are virtually unadulterated by anything man-made. It's a rare treat. It's also an opportunity see what the Casner Family saw when they moved cattle from Oak Creek to the high mesa at the end of this trail. The views haven't changed at all since then. And neither has the steep and challenging grade.

Overall, this is a tough trail, despite its relatively short distance. But if you take it slowly, you'll eventually come to an old wooden gate that marks the turnaround point. You can also continue a few hundred yards up to the top of the mesa, but the best views are in the other direction. Enjoy them on the way down. It's Mother Nature's reward for making it across her moat.

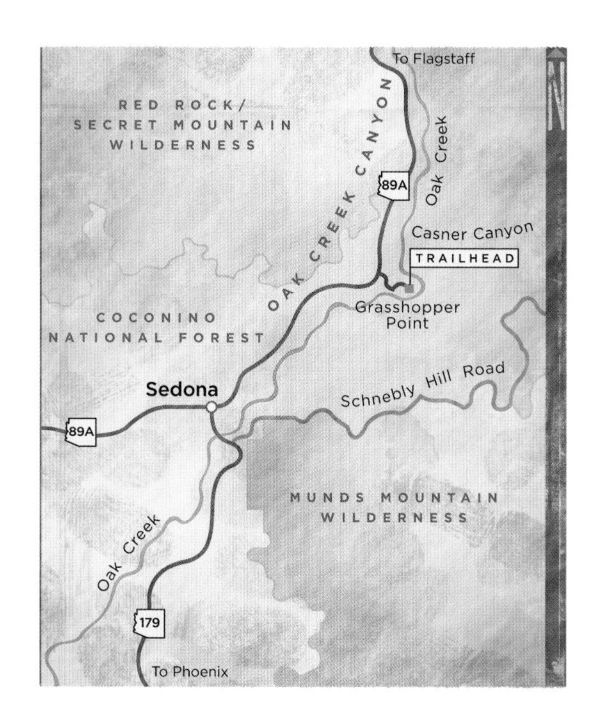

14 | TRAIL GUIDE

Length: 5 miles round-trip
Difficulty: Strenuous
Elevation: 4,396 to 5,912 feet
Trailhead GPS: N 34°53.233', W 111°43.869'
Directions: From the roundabout junction of State Route 179 and State Route 89A in Sedona, drive north on SR 89A for 2.4 miles to the Grasshopper Point parking lot on the right side of the highway.
Special Consideration: A $5 Red Rock parking pass is required along the highway; a $10 per vehicle (up to 5 people) fee is required in the Grasshopper Point parking area.
Vehicle Requirements: None; accessible by all vehicles
Dogs Allowed: Yes (on a leash)
USGS Map: Munds Park
Information: Red Rock Ranger District, 928-282-4119 or www.fs.fed.us/r3/coconino

Aspen Peak Trail

Hualapai Mountain Park | Kingman

Even if your idea of heading into the backcountry is going from Park Avenue to Central Park, you can handle this trail. It's not as easy as walking down the sidewalk, but in terms of "roughing it," this is about as benign as it gets. Of all the hikes in this book, this one best qualifies as a walk in the park. There are a couple reasons for that: 1) The trail is located within Hualapai Mountain Park, a spectacular and little-known area southeast of Kingman that's as diverse as any other sky island in Arizona; and 2) the trail was built by the Civilian Conservation Corps in 1937. As a general rule, the best trails in America were built by the CCC. They were built to last, and the Aspen Peak Trail is a prime example.

Although this hike is listed as the Aspen Peak Trail, it's really a combination of three trails: Aspen Springs, Potato Patch Loop and Aspen Peak. To get to the trail that takes you to the top, you'll first have to navigate the other two. And that's not a hardship. Overall, the three trails pass through four different life zones: chaparral, pine/oak, mixed conifer and fir/aspen.

The trek begins with the Aspen Springs Trail in Sawmill Canyon, a lush riparian area of Arizona walnuts, canyon maples and various species of oaks. The climb is gradual, with mild switchbacks and a wide path that accommodates horses. A few minutes into the hike you'll notice a significant depression in the hillside above. This is a remnant of the old Silver Bell Mine, which was first worked by prospectors in the 1870s and eventually

The Aspen Peak Trail offers panoramic views as it makes its way to the Dean Peak Overlook. | LARRY LINDAHL

Aspen Peak is the high point of the park's hiking trails, which were built by the Civilian Conservation Corps. | LARRY LINDAHL

shut down in 1994. Just beyond the mine is a spot known as the Kingman Overlook, from which you can see the city below and the distant Cerbat Mountains.

Along with the panoramas and the rocks and the trees, you'll notice that this trail often parallels and intersects a dirt road. Don't be confused. The dirt road is not the trail. It's used for horses and high-clearance vehicles. Stay on the trail, which, at this point, climbs through an open forest of ponderosa pines, New Mexican locusts and Gambel oaks. Then, as the Aspen Springs Trail approaches its intersection with the Potato Patch Loop, you'll start seeing Douglas firs and white firs. Massive granite boulders are also among the highlights as you make your way uphill.

In all, it takes about a half-hour to reach the Potato Patch Loop, which gets its name from the potatoes that were farmed commercially in a nearby canyon around 1910. Like the Silver Bell Mine, the potato fields are gone, but the trail is going strong.

At the intersection of the Aspen Springs Trail and the Potato Patch Loop, turn right and follow the loop in a counterclockwise direction — the Aspen Peak Trail is still about a mile away. After 10 minutes you'll come to a giant evergreen lying on its side. Without a doubt, this tree made a noise when it fell in the woods, even if no one was there to hear it. Just beyond the big tree is a rock formation known as the Three Gossips, along with a small grove of aspens.

From there, the loop continues uphill, past the Music Mountains Overlook, to a point where it joins the dirt road. The trail parallels the road

The trails in Hualapai Mountain Park were renovated in 1981 by a group of 10 Kingman teenagers, after originally being built in the 1930s by the Civilian Conservation Corps. After becoming unusable because of neglect, the trails were completely renovated over an 8-week summer session by the teens, who belonged to the Youth Conservation Corps. What a great way to spend a summer vacation.

for about 100 yards to its intersection with the Aspen Peak Trail, which is a short (0.6 miles) side trip that leads to the Dean Peak Overlook. This is as high as you can go on an established trail, but if you're a peak-bagger, you can scramble a few hundred feet more to the top of Aspen Peak.

Enjoy the views, and then retrace your steps back to the Potato Patch Loop. When you get there, turn left and continue in a counterclockwise direction. Within a short distance, the trail joins the dirt road again. The route gets a little tricky at this point. Look left for a large concrete-block building and follow the road in that direction. The structure is part of a Boy Scout (Troop 29) campsite. The road winds through the camp and reconnects with the loop trail about 15 minutes later.

Back on the trail, you'll notice that the vegetation has changed once again. Because this is the south side of the mountain, things are drier, which means that ponderosas, Gambel oaks and manzanitas predominate. It's prime habitat for mule deer and elk, so have your camera handy. Eventually, the Potato Patch Loop circles back to its connecting point with the Aspen Springs Trail, which takes you to the trailhead. By the time you get there, you'll feel a little burn in your legs and your lungs, but nothing too severe. This is, after all, just a walk in the park.

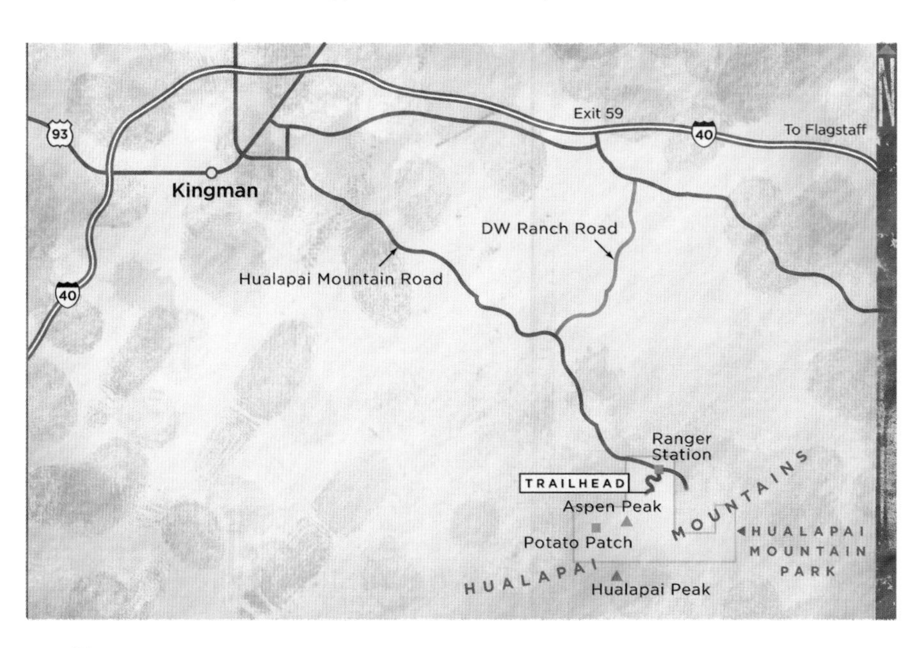

Length: 5.5 miles round-trip
Difficulty: Moderate
Elevation: 6,710 to 7,919 feet
Trailhead GPS: N 35°05.795', W 113°53.378'
Directions: From Kingman, drive east on Interstate 40 for 6 miles to Exit 59. From there, drive south on DW Ranch Road for 4.5 miles to Hualapai Mountain Road, turn left and continue 4 miles to the Hualapai Mountain Park Ranger Station. The trailhead is just off the main park road, about 0.75 miles inside the park. Ask the ranger for details.
Special Consideration: A $5 per vehicle entrance fee is required.
Vehicle Requirements: None; accessible by all vehicles
Dogs Allowed: Yes (on a leash)
USGS Map: Hualapai Peak
Information: Hualapai Mountain Park, 928-681-5700 or www.mcparks.com

Bass Canyon-Hot Springs Loop

Muleshoe Ranch | Galiuro Mountains

In the movie *Tombstone* — the 1993 version starring Val Kilmer — Charlton Heston plays Henry Hooker, a wealthy rancher who gives refuge to Doc Holliday while Wyatt Earp rides off for an epic showdown with Johnny Ringo. In real life, Henry Hooker was a wealthy rancher who bought a chunk of land originally homesteaded by Glendy King. King was a pioneer, and also an entrepreneur of sorts. His most notorious vision was to open a spa on his land in the early 1880s, which he did. As unlikely as a spa in the middle of nowhere in the days of Geronimo might sound, the property included a natural hot spring, which was enough to draw people in. However, as in all good Westerns, King was eventually gunned down and his homestead fell into the hands of Henry Hooker. Years later, it was obtained by The Nature Conservancy.

Today, the Hooker Hot Springs are still enjoyed by guests who make their way to the Conservancy's Muleshoe Ranch. The property includes a handful of casitas, and they're worth every penny if you can book one. In the springtime in particular, this is one of the most beautiful places in the world to spend a night. However, even if the No Vacancy sign is out, it's still a great place to explore. In addition to an incredible amount of wildlife — deer, squirrels, coatimundis, javelinas, foxes, coyotes, six species of hummingbirds, seven species of owls, and 14 species of hawks and eagles — the preserve protects seven permanently flowing streams, and the combined 12 miles of running water provides some of the best remaining

The view of the Galiuro Mountains is breathtaking from Jackson Cabin Road when the light is low and the clouds hint of rain. | TOM VEZO

Hackberry trees and mesquite trees thrive around Muleshoe Ranch. | JACK DYKINGA

aquatic habitat in the Southwest. The easiest way to experience this lush habitat is along the Bass Canyon-Hot Springs Loop.

The trail begins at The Nature Conservancy visitors center. From there, walk up the driveway to the gate you passed on your way in, turn left, and continue for 300 yards to Jackson Cabin Road. This is a four-wheel-drive dirt road, so you might encounter a vehicle or two, but it's highly unlikely. The loop trail follows this road for about a mile, and after 15 minutes you'll get some terrific 360-degree views of the surrounding mountains. The best views, perhaps, are behind you, looking back toward the ranch. Just beyond this viewpoint, you'll top a ridge and get even better views into Bass Canyon. At the bottom of the hill, a wooden sign marks the day-use area and the trailhead.

Before you begin your trek into the canyon, keep in mind that there isn't an actual trail. Because of the floods that race down Bass Creek, it's impossible to maintain a path. That's the nature of Mother Nature. That said, The Nature Conservancy does a terrific job of marking the route with blue ribbons, which seems appropriate. This is, without a doubt, one of Arizona's blue-ribbon trails.

As you make your way along the stream, the thing that'll strike you most is the enormity of the canyon's cottonwood trees. Named for the cotton-like mass surrounding their seeds, cottonwoods play a leading role in any Arizona riparian area, providing food, water and shelter. The food and shelter contributions are obvious, but the trees also provide water. Indirectly. Because of the shade they provide, evaporation is greatly decreased, which is good for every living thing in a riparian area. Sadly, the

Muleshoe Ranch was extremely popular among the wealthy set in the 1890s, and in one summer season alone, nearly 400 guests made the journey. While there, they enjoyed croquet, lawn tennis, billiards, horseback riding and hunting. Today, Muleshoe Ranch is operated by The Nature Conservancy, in partnership with the Bureau of Land Management and the U.S. Forest Service, and spans 49,120 acres of rugged semidesert grasslands, with five original 1800s casitas used for lodging.

cottonwood makes up the fastest-depleting forest in the United States. Admire them as you pass by. Ditto for the Arizona sycamores. They're all spectacular.

After about a mile of bushwhacking through the gorgeous preserve, you'll come to Pipeline Road, just beyond which is the intersection of Bass Canyon and Hot Springs Canyon. You can't miss the junction. It's wide open and especially sandy. Although Hot Springs Wash is usually dry at this junction, you'll start seeing water again as you get closer to the ranch headquarters. To get there, simply hang a left and follow the wash to complete the loop. Like Bass Canyon, Hot Springs Canyon doesn't have an established trail, but as long as you hug the wash, you can chart your own course. As usual, be aware of weather conditions and the possibility of flash floods — in addition to the requisite hiking gear, you also need a state-of-the-art thinking cap when trekking in the wilderness.

The hike up Hot Springs Wash will take about an hour, and along the way you'll intersect the Muleshoe Preserve Nature Trail and the Vista Trail, a route for horses. You can detour onto either one, or continue up the wash. Either way, you'll get where you're going, and if you're lucky enough to have room reservations at the ranch, Henry Hooker's hot springs will be waiting. They make a perfect ending to a blue-ribbon hike.

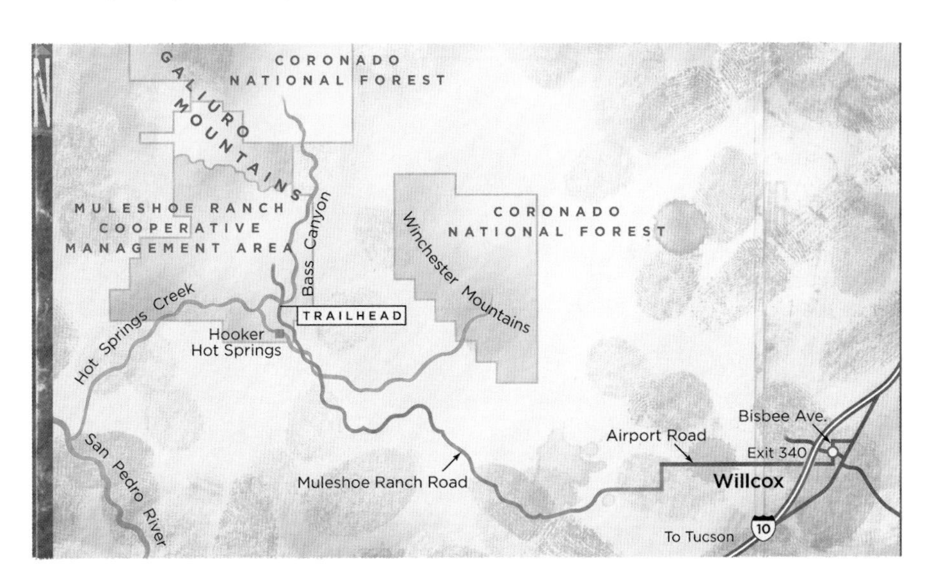

Length: 3.5 miles round-trip
Difficulty: Easy
Elevation: 4,087 to 4,200 feet
Trailhead GPS: N 32°20.302', W 110°14.296'
Directions: From Tucson, take Interstate 10 east for 80 miles to Willcox. Exit in Willcox onto Rex Allen Drive. At the first traffic light, bear right onto N. Bisbee Avenue, and then turn right onto Airport Road. Follow Airport Road for 15 miles to its junction with Muleshoe Ranch Road (look for a row of mailboxes), turn right and continue 14 miles to the ranch headquarters.
Vehicle Requirements: High-clearance and four-wheel-drive required after heavy rains
Dogs Allowed: Yes (on a leash)
USGS Maps: Soza Mesa, Hookers Hot Springs
Information: The Nature Conservancy, 520-212-4295 or www.nature.org/arizona

17

Bell Trail

Wet Beaver Wilderness | Sedona

This is one of those trails the locals like to keep to themselves for fear it'll be inundated by city mice looking for an adventure in the country. However, unlike the Colonel's recipe, the secret's out. It's been out. Nevertheless, this trail is never too crowded. You won't be alone, but you won't be stuck in a conga line of urbanites, either.

The trailhead is located a stone's throw from the Sedona exit off Interstate 17. Actually, there are two trailheads, which can be a little confusing. The first option is the Bruce Brockett Trailhead, which is named for the late poet, politician and cattleman who owned the surrounding V Bar V Ranch. As you're driving east on Forest Road 618, you'll see a sign for "trailer parking." If you turn left, a short dirt road will take you to the trailhead. Although

The Bell Trail, which parallels Wet Beaver Creek, is doable any time of year. | LARRY LINDAHL

Hikers along the Bell Trail will experience the riparian nature of Wet Beaver Creek. | NICK BEREZENKO

this location is used primarily by folks with horses, hikers are welcome, too — from the lot, there's a short connector trail that leads to the Bell Trail. The better option, however, is a quarter-mile beyond the Brockett turnoff.

Again, turn left onto a short dirt road. The trailhead, which is located just over the ridge, is more traditional, with restroom facilities and plenty of parking. Whichever lot you choose, as you look around, you'll see why Bruce Brockett sank his roots into this spectacular red dirt. It's beautiful country.

Like many of the trails around Sedona, the Bell Trail is doable any time of year. In the summer, Wet Beaver Creek, which parallels the trail, offers

Toward the end of the Bell Trail you'll see what the locals affectionately refer to as "The Crack." It's a natural pool that made it into *National Geographic: Adventure* magazine as one of the nation's best swimming holes. In addition to an unfair amount of scenic beauty, The Crack features a spectacular rock ledge that's used as a hangout by adventurous visitors. A word to the wise: Don't explore The Crack in the nude. Rangers have been known to give out tickets.

cool relief from the searing heat. During the other three seasons, including spring, the creek is just another incentive — with or without the water, this trek is one of the best in the book.

The trail kicks off on a wide gravel path that eventually narrows down, but is never hard to follow. Although it doesn't intersect the creek until Bell's Crossing, there are a number of side trails that'll take you down to the water, which runs year-round and is home to smallmouth bass and trout.

Before too long you'll see a large dead cottonwood. Just beyond the tree, look up to the left at the hillside of prickly pears. If the sun is shining, and it's the right time of day, the cactuses will appear as if they've been rigged with fiber optics. It's quite a sight.

After another mile or so of meandering, the trail leads to the boundary of Wet Beaver Wilderness Area, which was established in 1984 and encompasses 6,000 acres. The Weir Trail veers to the right at this point; the Bell Trail continues toward the east. As you head that way, look up, down, left or right, and you'll get an eyeful. Eventually, the trail climbs to a narrow bench that runs along the canyon's north wall. It's a perfect place to kick back, listen to the creek and eat some Goldfish crackers. A PB&J would work, as well.

From there, the path drops down to the canyon bottom, where it finally fords the creek at Bell's Crossing. Although the trail continues for another 1.5 miles uphill to the south rim of the canyon, this is the obvious turnaround point. In the summer, it's where you'll take your shoes off. In the spring, it's simply another dose of the great outdoors — the ultimate incentive.

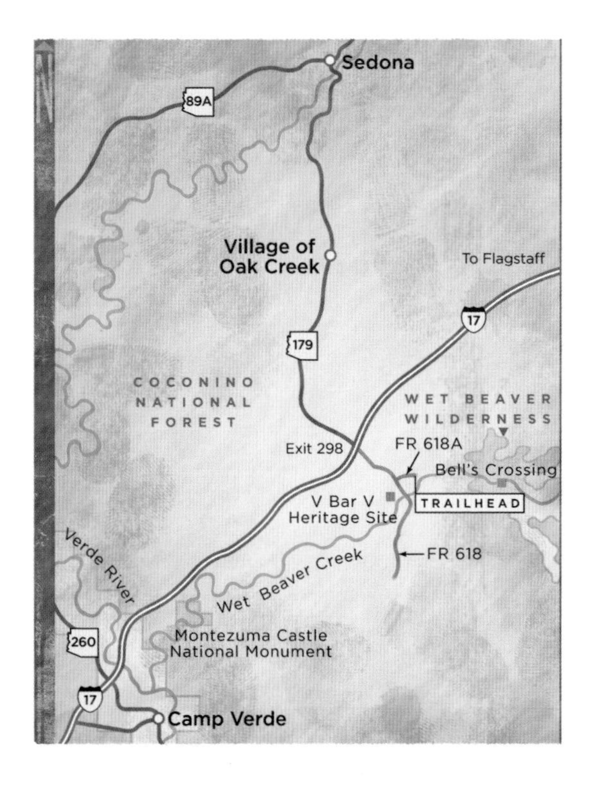

17 | TRAIL GUIDE

Length: 6.6 miles round-trip (to Bell's Crossing)
Difficulty: Easy
Elevation: 3,849 to 4,115 feet
Trailhead GPS: N 34°40.468', W 111°42.796'
Directions: From Phoenix, take Interstate 17 north to the Sedona exit (Exit 298) and turn right onto Forest Road 618. Take FR 618 for 2 miles to Forest Road 618A, turn left and continue a quarter-mile to the trailhead parking lot.
Vehicle Requirements: None; accessible by all vehicles
Dogs Allowed: Yes (on a leash)
USGS Maps: Casner Butte, Walker Mountain
Information: Red Rock Ranger District, 928-282-4119 or www.fs.fed.us/r3/coconino

18

Bright Angel Trail

South Rim | Grand Canyon National Park

If you're looking for a solo expedition, this isn't it — at least 100,000 people a year make this trek, and maybe a half-million more hike portions of it. If, however, you want to experience one of the most renowned trails in the world, the Bright Angel awaits. But before you lace up, you need to be prepared. The National Park Service strongly advises against doing this trail as a day hike, but it is doable. If you're going to heed the advice of the NPS, you'll need reservations at Phantom Ranch or one of the nearby campgrounds (Indian Garden or Bright Angel). Either way, you'll also need plenty of food and water, and exceptional cardiovascular health. Check with your doctor and the backcountry office for all of the specifics.

The trail begins just beyond the historic Kolb Studio on the South Rim. The trees you'll see are mostly piñons and junipers, some of which are more than 100 years old. Almost immediately, you'll come to the first of two tunnels. As you pass through, look up to the left. The pictographs are known as Mallery's Grotto. They were painted by members of various Indian civilizations over several centuries. The second tunnel is just beyond the first. From there, the trail switchbacks to the Mile-and-a-Half Resthouse. As the name suggests, you'll have gone 1.5 miles at this point, but geologically, you'll have traveled for millions of years.

Moving on, you'll quickly come to the Three-Mile Resthouse and a series of switchbacks known as Jacob's Ladder. While you're winding

The Bright Angel Trail begins on the South Rim of the Grand Canyon and passes through Indian Garden before winding down to the Colorado River. | NICK BEREZENKO

Mule trains are a common sight on the Bright Angel Trail, which is one of the best-known hikes in the world. | TOM BROWNOLD

down, take a moment to look up. California condors, which disappeared from the area in 1925, were reintroduced in 1996. On a good day, you might see one or two or more of these endangered species soaring in the sky. It's a remarkable a sight.

The approximate halfway point of the trail is Indian Garden, a spring-fed oasis that was used for centuries by Ancestral Puebloans, and later, into the 20th century, by the Havasupai Indians. For day-hikers, this is the most common turnaround point, although some explorers also make the trek out to nearby Plateau Point, a short and easy side trip that offers excellent views of the Inner Gorge of the Canyon.

If you're continuing down to the river, you'll pass through Garden Creek upon leaving Indian Garden. This area, too, was used by Ancestral Puebloans, who raised corn, beans and squash. Today, it's another refreshing respite on a long journey that continues to the Devil's Corkscrew. The

The Bright Angel Trail was named one of America's "10 Most Dangerous Hikes" by *Backpacker* magazine. The reason is obvious: Canyon temperatures routinely top 110° F in the summer, and that heat, combined with the exertion of climbing almost 4,500 vertical feet over 9.5 miles, results in about 200 heat-related rescues in the park each year, most of them on the Bright Angel Trail. The trail's name originated with Major John Wesley Powell on his pioneering exploration of the Colorado River in 1869. Powell regretted having named a muddy creek upstream the "Dirty Devil." So, when he later found a creek with sparkling clear water, he gave it the more reverent name, "Bright Angel," after a character in Milton's *Paradise Lost*.

lengthy set of switchbacks zigzag through a vast rock formation known as the Vishnu schist. In this zone, the vegetation changes from the riparian habitat along the stream to a drier, desert region. It changes back, however, once you reach Columbine Spring, which seeps from a cliff to the left of the trail. The rest of the route follows Pipe Creek to the Colorado River. This is where the Bright Angel Trail connects with the River Trail.

A mule deer scampers among the redbud trees at Indian Garden Campground. | TOM BROWNOLD

The latter, which was constructed by the Civilian Conservation Corps in the mid-1930s, parallels the river for about 1.5 miles to Silver Bridge, where it crosses the Colorado River and leads to Bright Angel Campground. Phantom Ranch is just a little farther down. Either place makes a great place to spend the night. But don't show up without reservations. The rooms and campsites book up as much as a year in advance. When you share a trail with 100,000 people, that's the reality. It's worth the extra planning, though. Bright Angel is justifiably one of the most renowned trails in the world.

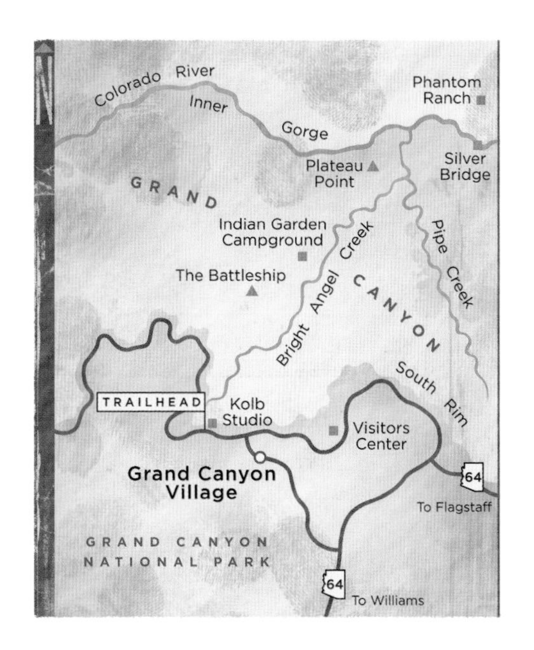

18 | TRAIL GUIDE

Length: 19.2 miles round-trip
Difficulty: Strenuous
Elevation: 6,860 to 2,400 feet
Trailhead GPS: N 36°03.473', W 112°08.556'
Directions: From the South Rim entrance station, follow S. Entrance Road for about 8 miles as it winds around to the west end of the South Rim's Grand Canyon Village. The Bright Angel trailhead is on the right, just beyond Kolb Studio.
Special Consideration: National Park Service fees apply.
Vehicle Requirements: None; accessible by all vehicles
Dogs Allowed: No
USGS Maps: Bright Angel, Grand Canyon, Phantom Ranch
Information: Backcountry Office, Grand Canyon National Park, 928-638-7888 or www.nps.gov/grca

Grandview Trail

South Rim | Grand Canyon National Park

You could spend a lifetime hiking the Grand Canyon and never see it all. Most people don't have that kind of time, so they tackle the Bright Angel Trail (see page 94) or one of the Kaibabs (see page 210). They're spectacular routes, they're easy to get to and there's no downside to hiking them. Figuratively. The literal downside is amazing. Another great option is the Grandview Trail, which connects with the Tonto Trail and eventually drops all the way down to the Colorado River. Most hikers, however, go only as far as Horseshoe Mesa, which is the halfway point between the rim and the river, and that's where this hike ends up.

The trail begins at Grandview Point, which, at 7,400 feet, is the highest point on the South Rim. In addition to serving as the trailhead for this hike, the point is popular with drive-by tourists. Back in 1897, however, it was much more than that. That's when miner Pete Berry turned his log home into the two-story Grandview Hotel. At the time, El Tovar was still a few years away, which made Berry's place the premier destination on the South Rim. However, once El Tovar was constructed and the railroad built a line to Grand Canyon Village, the Grandview Hotel faded into the landscape. Fortunately for hikers, the trail did not.

Although the park service doesn't maintain the trail on a regular basis, it's in good shape — especially since the upper switchbacks were repaired in 2005 after a massive rockslide destroyed several sections of the trail.

The Grandview Trail connects to the Tonto Trail and offers this view of Wotans Throne. | NICK BEREZENKO

The Grandview Trail isn't as popular as other Grand Canyon hikes, but the views are equally impressive. | NICK BEREZENKO

Bottom line: You won't have to worry about the trail, just your conditioning. In the short 3.1 miles to Horseshoe Mesa, the trail drops nearly 2,500 vertical feet, and the abrupt descent begins the instant you set foot on the trail. The switchbacks, which can be icy in the spring, demand that you look where you're going. It's a tall order, considering the views in front of you, but you need to be careful. The most dangerous switches are near the top.

Heading down, you'll be exposed to the sun, except in a few pockets shaded by a handful of Douglas firs — they're remnants of a forest that covered the area during the last Ice Age. After about 30 minutes, you'll come to the Coconino Saddle, which rises up from the side canyons created by Hance and Cottonwood creeks. The saddle is shaded and makes a great place to sit and gaze. It's also an ideal turnaround point for people not equipped to make the full run to the mesa.

Leaving the saddle, the trail takes a break from the descent, levels off for a few hundred yards, and cuts through a stand of trees. This is one of the best parts of the trail, but the level ground doesn't last for long. Five minutes later, the steep descent begins again, and what you'll notice is that going downhill can be very fatiguing. It almost makes you look forward to going up. *Until you're going up.*

With the exception of some minor boulder-scrambling about an hour into the hike, the terrain remains the same. There's sensory overload, of course, with the Seventh Natural Wonder at your fingertips, but don't forget to look toward your toes from time to time, too. In the springtime, wildflowers are coming to life in the Canyon. Look for Palmer lupines, scarlet buglers and globemallows. In an environment like the Grand Canyon, it's hard to stand out, but the delicate wildflowers do just that. They're exceptionally beautiful.

When miners Pete Berry and Ralph and Niles Cameron were setting up shop on Horseshoe Mesa, they knew they'd need a good trail up to the South Rim, so they built the Grandview Trail in 1893. Among the many loads that were hauled up the trail was a 700-pound copper nugget. It took six men six days to make that trek. Once on top, the ore sample was shipped to the 1893 Chicago World's Fair, where it assayed at 70 percent copper and won first prize in one of the mineral competitions.

Eventually, after 31 switchbacks and the incineration of up to a thousand calories, you'll arrive on the mesa. You'll know you're there when the views open up to your left and right — it's a 270-degree panorama. Once you're on the mesa, you'll quickly come to an old tree wrapped with rusted barbed-wire. It's the first remnant you'll see from the Last Chance Mine, which was developed in 1890 by Pete Berry and Ralph and Niles Cameron. You'll also see old tin cans, fragments of copper ore (green malachite and blue azurite) and the red-rock ruins of an old cookhouse.

Back in its heyday, the mining camp included a blacksmith forge, corrals and a bunkhouse. Those are gone today, but campsites do exist (a backcountry permit is required), as well as eco-friendly toilets. They come in handy, but if you need privacy, you'll have to hold it. Although the toilets have short walls on three sides, there's no roof and no door — the brave souls who enter the facility sit facing into the open.

The iffy privy notwithstanding, Horseshoe Mesa is a remarkable place to visit. History, geology, ecology ... it's all right there, along with several short spur trails. If your legs are willing, they're worth exploring. However, keep in mind that the return trip is exponentially more difficult than the trip down. Like the Bright Angel Trail and the Kaibabs, the hike out will wipe you out. It's worth it, though. That's the nature of the Grand Canyon.

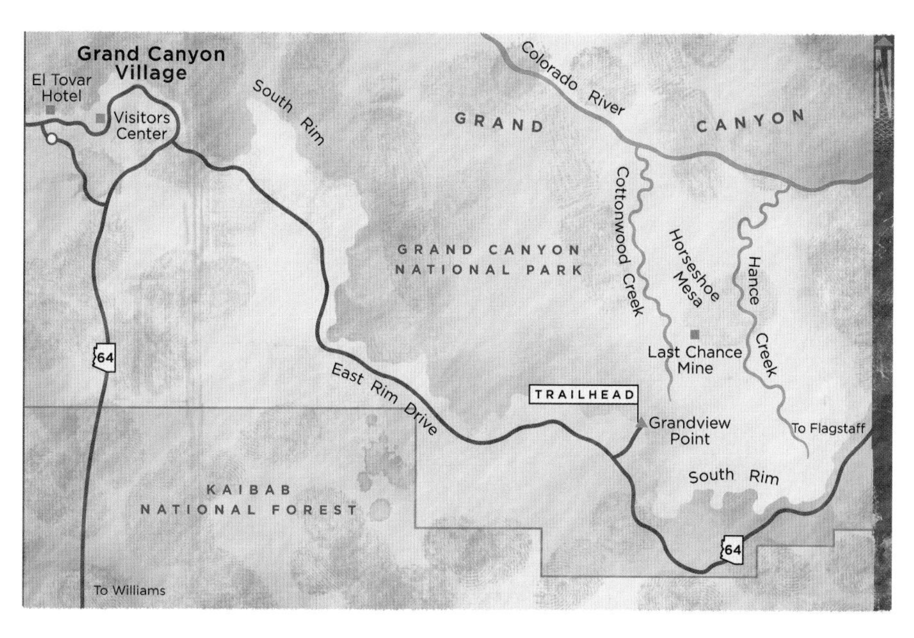

Length: 6.2 miles round-trip (to Horseshoe Mesa)
Difficulty: Strenuous
Elevation: 7,406 to 4,932 feet
Trailhead GPS: N 35°59.908', W 111°59.260'
Directions: From Grand Canyon Village on the South Rim, drive 12 miles east on East Rim Drive to Grandview Point. The trailhead is well marked.

Special Consideration: National Park Service fees apply.
Vehicle Requirements: None; accessible by all vehicles
Dogs Allowed: No
USGS Map: Grandview Point
Information: Backcountry Office, Grand Canyon National Park, 928-638-7888 or www.nps.gov/grca

Green Mountain Trail

Santa Catalina Mountains | Coronado National Forest

Vermont has the Green Mountains. It's a beautiful range that includes a premier ski resort and a long stretch of the Appalachian Trail. In New England, green is everywhere. That's one of the things that makes the region so appealing. Most people think green is unheard of in Arizona. But despite the stereotype that it's nothing but a desert wasteland, Arizona actually ranks third among all U.S. states in terms of biodiversity. Among other things, there's plenty of green, and there's even a Green Mountain. It's not as well known as the one in Vermont, but it's scenic in its own right, and you won't need snowshoes to hike it in the spring.

The Green Mountain Trail is one of many great options in the Santa Catalina Mountains. Like other nearby trails, this one can be done as a one-way hike using a car-shuttle system, or as a round-tripper. The upper trailhead is located at the San Pedro Vista and the lower trailhead is at the General Hitchcock Campground. For this listing, the route begins up top at San Pedro, where there's a good-sized parking lot. The trail itself begins on the east side of the lot behind a metal trailhead sign. Finding the trail can be a little tricky because of the large number of well-worn pathways that radiate from the parking area. But if you follow the rough rock steps up the slope, you'll see that all of the routes eventually merge into one.

Within a few minutes, the main trail intersects a side trail that leads to the top of Green Mountain. Stay left and gear up for a series of steep switchbacks that pass by another side trail (Brush Corral) and wind around the mountain for which the trail is named.

The Green Mountain Trail can be hiked one way with a car shuttle. | RANDY PRENTICE

The Green Mountain Trail is popular with mountain-bikers and hikers alike. | RANDY PRENTICE

Up to this point, the surrounding forest is primarily ponderosa pines and Douglas firs. It's lush and green. Moving on, the evergreens are replaced by oaks, manzanitas, yuccas and beargrass. The change is noticeable, and so are the spectacular views to the northeast. This is a good place to use the "panoramic" setting on your camera.

After about 30 minutes, you'll come to another spur of the Brush Corral Trail. Stay right and keep your ears tuned for the sounds of mountain bikers. Although Bob Marley used to sing, "my feet is my only carriage," not everyone travels that way, mon. Hard-core bikers love the downhill run of the Green Mountain Trail, and it's a good idea to step aside when you hear them coming.

From that intersection, the trail switchbacks uphill over some rocks and boulders, including two massive cornerstones that serve as trail sentries. Just beyond them is yet another trail intersection (Maverick Springs) and a formation known as Bear Saddle, which sits at an elevation

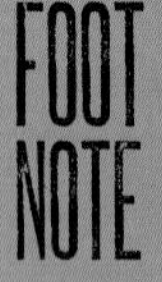

Nearby Pusch Ridge was named for pioneer George Pusch, who came to Arizona from Germany in the 1870s. In 1874, he established the Steam Pump Ranch near the base of the ridge. At the time, it was one of the largest cattle ranches in the Arizona Territory. In 1978, the Pusch Ridge Wilderness Area was created to preserve and protect the dwindling desert bighorn sheep population in the area. However, due to increased residential and commercial development, the sheep population has decreased dramatically. The last documented sighting was in 2005.

of 6,950 feet and serves as the head of Bear Canyon. At the saddle, the route can be a little confusing. Your instincts will tell you to veer slightly left; however, that's the wrong way — that route is a secondary trail that leads to Guthrie Mountain. Instead, you'll want to make an almost 90-degree turn to the right. This is the continuation of the Green Mountain Trail, which follows Bear Canyon for just under 2 miles to the General Hitchcock Campground. This homestretch is probably the most beautiful part of the trail. The scenic vistas will have disappeared, but you'll be surrounded, once again, by ponderosas and Douglas firs, as well as Arizona cypress. You'll also cross over a series of large flat rocks reminiscent of something you might see on the Paria Plateau in Northern Arizona.

Eventually, after several crossings of Bear Creek, which could be running in the spring, and passing some mammoth ponderosas, the trail bottoms out and parallels the wash to the campground. As you approach on the pine-needle-cushioned footpath, veer toward the 20-foot-tall concrete water tank and look for the notches on the trees and the nearby trailhead sign. The campground will be obvious, but you'll need this bearing for the return trip. Before you take off, park yourself at one of the picnic tables, refuel, and enjoy the lush green forest around you. It's not Vermont, but it sure could be.

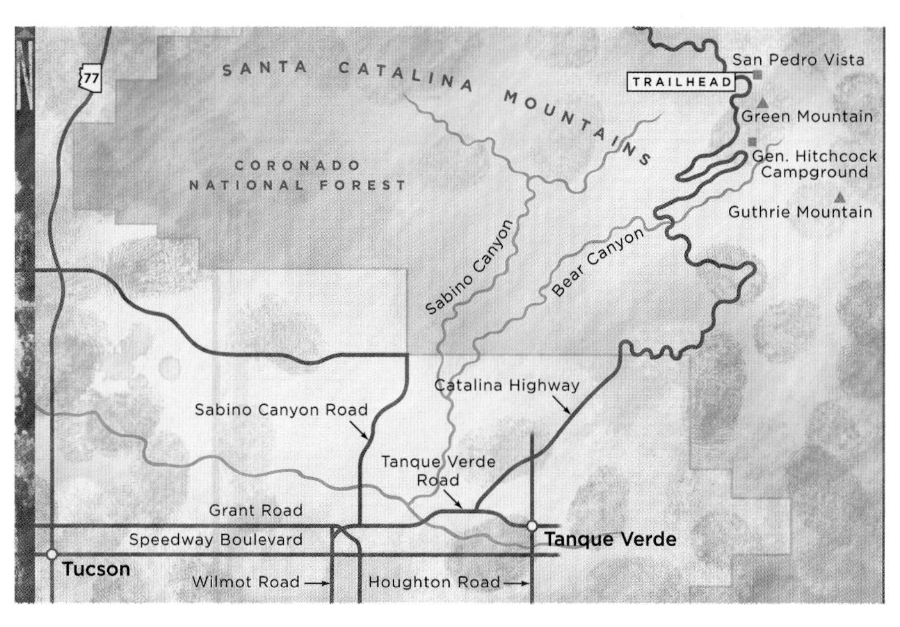

Length: 7.8 miles round-trip
Difficulty: Moderate
Elevation: 6,000 to 7,300 feet
Trailhead GPS: N 32°24.007', W 110°41.404'
Directions: From Tanque Verde Road in Tucson, drive 4.2 miles on the Catalina Highway to the Forest Service boundary and continue 17.5 miles to the San Pedro Vista.

Special Consideration: A $5 day pass (per vehicle) is required.
Vehicle Requirements: None; accessible by all vehicles
Dogs Allowed: Yes (on a leash)
USGS Map: Mount Bigelow
Information: Santa Catalina Ranger District, 520-749-8700 or www.fs.fed.us/r3/coronado

21

Heart of Rocks Loop

Chiricahua National Monument

The Apaches called them "standing up rocks." Today, people call them hoodoos or pinnacles or the most amazing rock formations they've ever seen. All of the above will work when referring to the centerpiece of Chiricahua National Monument.

Quick science lesson: The origin of the pinnacles began 27 million years ago, when eruptions from the Turkey Creek Volcano spewed ash over a 1,200-square-mile area that included the present-day monument. The ash particles melted together and formed layers of rhyolite, which was slowly eroded by ice and water. What remains are the "standing up rocks" that make this park unique. Although the hoodoos can be photographed from any car window, the most impressive rocks can be seen only on the Heart of Rocks

From the Heart of Rocks Loop, you can catch one of Arizona's fabled sunsets. | PAUL GILL

Loop, which can be reached in a number of ways. For this hike, you'll start at the monument's visitors center.

To get to the loop, you'll first need to tackle two connector trails: Lower Rhyolite Canyon and Sarah Deming. The first is an easy-to-follow dirt path that's instantly recognizable as the handiwork of the Civilian Conservation Corps, which built the trail in 1934. The path parallels a small creek for 1.5 miles before its intersection with the Sarah Deming Trail. Along the way, views to the left are vintage Chiricahuas, with rows and rows of hoodoos, some as big as U-Haul trucks, set against an unbelievably blue sky. If Bob Ross were painting the scene, he'd use phthalo blue. Most of this stretch follows a gradual incline, but it's nothing strenuous.

In addition to the hoodoos, you might catch a glimpse of a coatimundi in the Chiricahuas. | BRUCE D. TAUBERT

After about a half-hour you'll come to the intersection with Sarah Deming. The Upper Rhyolite Trail veers left; you'll veer right. Unlike Rhyolite Canyon, which is fairly wide from side to side, Sarah Deming Canyon is narrow and more forested, and if the winter has brought some rain and snow, there's a good chance you'll hear water along much of this trail. The creek at the bottom of the canyon will make most of the noise, but even up on the trail itself you'll encounter some small springs that trickle across the path before heading 100 feet downhill to the main creek. In addition to the water, check out the two chimney-shaped rocks that look as if they were built of brick by stonemasons. They're huge. You can't miss them. Five minutes later, you'll cross the creek, veer left, and then switch right for the final ascent to the Heart of Rocks Loop.

Even before you get there, you'll start seeing some of the great shapes, and you'll find it hard to stop taking photos. Fortunately, the CCC carved steps into the trail, which makes it easy to look around and hike at the same time. In all, this uphill stretch takes about 15 minutes, after which you'll come to the loop. Of course, it doesn't matter which direction you go, but

The Chiricahua Mountains are at the junction of four major biological zones: 1) the Sonoran Desert of Arizona and Mexico, 2) the Chihuahuan Desert of Arizona, New Mexico, Texas and Mexico, 3) the southern Rocky Mountains, and 4) Mexico's Sierra Madre. This collision of bio zones gives the area a unique and extremely diverse population of flora and fauna.

the park service recommends clockwise, and that's how this hike is written.

There are many marvels within Chiricahua National Monument, including the fact that it's home to more than 1,000 plant species, the southernmost stand of Engelmann spruce trees in the United States, and an array of wildlife such as coatimundis, cougars, black bears and all four species of skunks native to Arizona — spotted, striped, hooded and hog-nosed. None of that, however, will seem more impressive than the hoodoos you'll be hiking through on this incredible loop. Among the many well-known rock formations you'll see are Totem Pole, Big Balanced Rock, and Punch and Judy. Thor's Hammer is there, too, and just beyond it is an amazing view of Cochise Head, a massive rock formation that looms in the distance.

Although the loop only takes about 25 minutes, you'll probably end up lingering and taking photos. It's also a good opportunity think about the history of the area. Long before the establishment of Chiricahua National Monument and the overlapping Chiricahua Wilderness Area, this was the home of the Apaches, including Cochise, Geronimo and others. As you look around, you'll understand why they settled in this environment. The "standing up rocks" make up one of the most amazing landscapes you'll ever see.

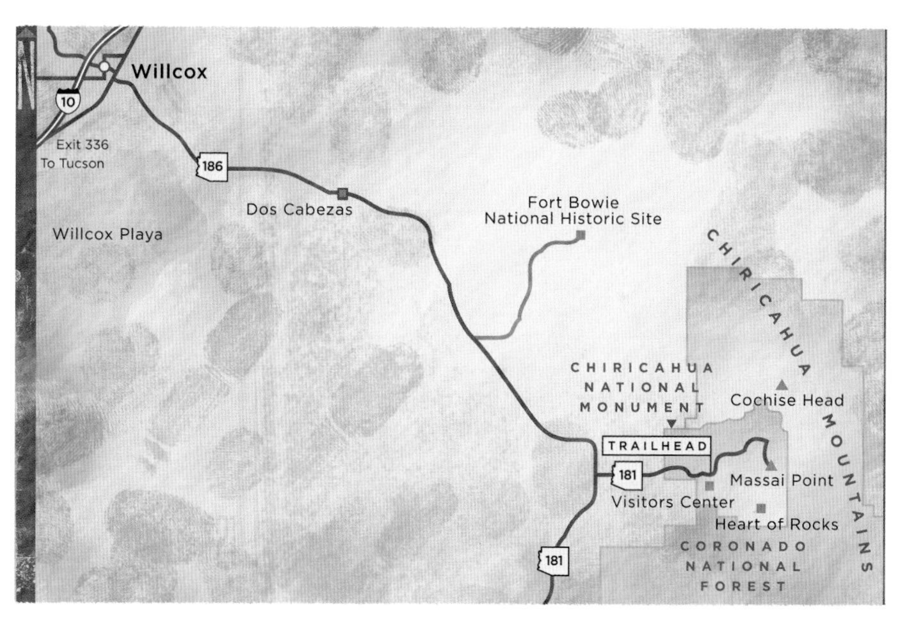

Length: 7 miles round-trip
Difficulty: Moderate
Elevation: 5,366 to 6,870 feet
Trailhead GPS: N 33°00.335', W 109°21.361'
Directions: From Tucson, take Interstate 10 east to the first Willcox exit. Veer right and drive 3 miles into town to the first stoplight. Turn right and follow State Route 186 for 32 miles to the junction of State Route 181. Turn left onto SR 181 and drive 4 miles to the Chiricahua National Monument entrance. The trailhead is located at the east end of the visitors center parking lot on Bonita Canyon Drive.
Special Consideration: National Park Service fees apply.
Vehicle Requirements: None; accessible by all vehicles
Dogs Allowed: No
USGS Map: Cochise Head
Information: Chiricahua National Monument, 520-824-3560 or www.nps.gov/chir

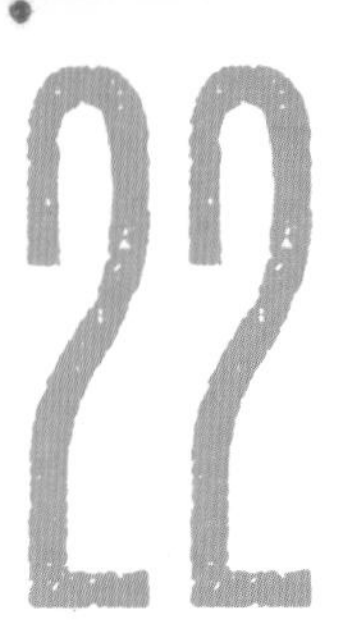

Hell's Hole Trail

Salome Wilderness | Tonto National Forest

If you're tired of people, and not just the revolving door of annoying celebrities who inundate the media, but people in general, then Hell's Hole is where you want to be. Although it sounds ironic that any part of hell is a better option than wherever it is you might be coming from, in this case, it is. Not only will you escape the crowds, but you'll also get away from Facebook, Twitter, e-mail, voice mail ... if ever there was a place that's off the grid, Hell's Hole is it.

The trail that leads to the hole is one of only two within the Salome Wilderness Area, which is one of the most scenic and least-visited areas in the state. The name, however, has no real connection to Arizona. It originated with Spanish-speaking settlers who named the nearby creek for the daughter of Herodias, the biblical character who was given the head of John the Baptist. Although the name was changed to "Sally May" in the 1880s by local pioneers, the Forest Service changed it back to Salome in 1927.

From the trailhead, which is located under the tall pines of Reynolds Creek Campground, the route begins a gradual uphill climb through the trees. Because the high end of the trail sits about a mile above sea level, snow is possible, even in the spring. As with any trail, it's always best to call the ranger station ahead of time and check on road and trail accessibility. Under normal conditions, this hike is perfect this time of year.

About 15 minutes into the hike you'll come to an impressive alligator

Very few hikers explore Hell's Hole, but those who do are treated to scenic beauty. | JEFF SNYDER

Hell's Hole is a strenous hike and one of only two trails in the Salome Wilderness. | JEFF SNYDER

juniper, followed by an equally impressive manzanita. Past them, the trail begins a downhill stretch through a thick forest of ponderosa pines and Douglas firs. Unlike some pine forests in Arizona, the ground cover in this wooded area is especially thick. And especially beautiful. Also, at this point at least, the trail is well-marked and easy to follow. By the end of the hike, things will be different.

Not to be outdone by the impressive juniper and manzanita, one of the largest ponderosas anywhere grabs your attention at the 30-minute mark. There are more pines farther along, but none quite like this. Eventually, the evergreens will give way to scrub oaks and piñons, and the views will open

Arizona has more place-names using the word "Hell" than any other state in the country, including seven spots named Hell's Hole — two within Tonto National Forest. There's also a Hell Hole in Booger Canyon, a Hell Hole Valley, two Hell's Hole Canyons, one Hell's Hole Creek and one Hell's Hole Peak. Historians attribute the names to the fact that most pioneers found Arizona's climate harsh and unforgiving. Or maybe they were just trying to be clever.

up, offering a good look at just how rugged this wilderness area is. As you make your way north, listen for the sounds of Workman Creek. It isn't visible at first, but you will hear it. Like Salome Creek, which runs east-west through the entire wilderness area, Workman Creek is a perennial stream that supports a decent population of brown trout and rainbow trout, and also serves as a lifeline for some of the area's wildlife, including bobcats, badgers, ringtails and coyotes.

After an hour, you'll arrive at the water. The riparian nature of Workman Creek makes it a great place to gear up for the rest of the hike, especially the descent into Hell's Hole. But first, you'll officially cross into the Salome Wilderness Area and begin a lengthy uphill climb. Along the way you'll pass an intersection with the Boyer Trail, the only other established trail in the wilderness. Veer right to stay on the Hell's Hole Trail, which crosses a muddy mesa that leads to some brutal switchbacks that take you down into the trail's namesake. Not only are the switchbacks steep — and more challenging on the way out — they're also overgrown with prickly brush, making it difficult to find the way. You don't have to be Magellan to navigate the mess, but you do have to pay attention. Sometimes, when you think you're supposed to go right, you need to go left. And vice versa. The bushwhacking is worth it, though.

By the time you get to the end of the trail, after almost 3 hours of hiking, you'll be greeted once again by Workman Creek. This time, though, it's in a deep canyon and the waterway is flooded with large boulders, some as big as Barcaloungers. You probably won't run into other people at the bottom, but if you do, they're likely like-minded — it takes a special hiker to hike into a place called Hell's Hole.

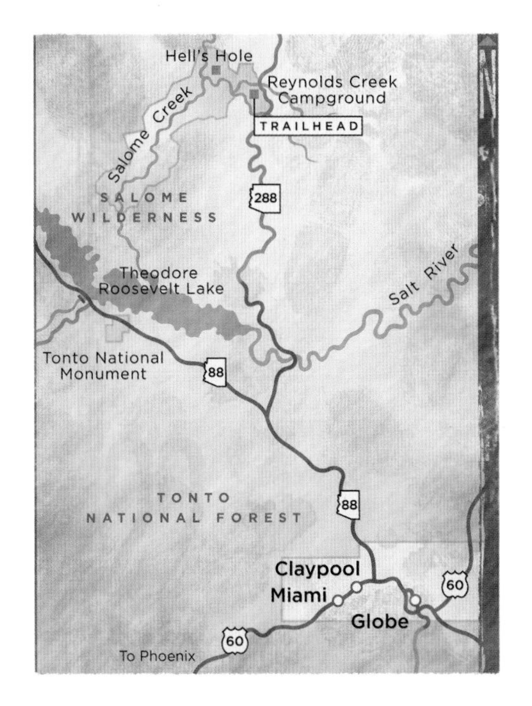

22 | TRAIL GUIDE

Length: 12 miles round-trip
Difficulty: Strenuous
Elevation: 3,920 to 5,480 feet
Trailhead GPS: N 33°52.262', W 110°58.511'
Directions: From Claypool, drive north on State Route 88 for approximately 15 miles to its junction with State Route 288. Continue north on SR 288 for 27 miles to the trailhead at Reynolds Creek Campground.
Vehicle Requirements: None; accessible by all vehicles
Dogs Allowed: Yes (on a leash)
USGS Maps: Armer Mountain, Copper Mountain, McFadden Peak
Information: Pleasant Valley Ranger District, 928-462-4300 or www.fs.fed.us/r3/tonto

Maxwell Trail

West Clear Creek Wilderness | Mogollon Rim

It takes anywhere from 80 to 100 years for an aluminum can to disappear on its own. They are, in a sense, biodegradable, but it takes *forever*. Cigarette butts last about 5 years. And even a banana peel can take up to 2 years. That's the first lesson you'll learn on the Maxwell Trail, courtesy of a yellow metal sign tacked to the information board at the trailhead. Everything else will be learned through the five senses. Well ... at least four of the five senses, anyway. Although Euell Gibbons used to say that many parts of a pine tree are edible, you really should pack your own snacks. Don't eat the pine trees.

The trail, which is located at the upper end of the West Clear Creek Wilderness Area, begins with a series of steep downhill switchbacks. Through the trees, you'll catch a glimpse of the lush canyon below, and looking ahead, you might be tempted to cut across the switchbacks. Don't. This is a sensitive area, and shortcutting destroys vegetation and causes erosion. Besides, there's no rush. This trail is short — less than a mile each way.

Like many trails on the Mogollon Rim, this one is rocky and loose in places. And it's steep, so be careful. After about 10 minutes of trekking, the canyon comes into full view. The rocks aren't as red as they are in Oak Creek Canyon, but Willow Canyon is clearly a not-so-distant cousin. There are shades of Walnut Canyon lineage, as well. About a minute later, stop and look up. You'll see an impressive rock wall over your right shoulder. The rocks above the rim are predominately limestone, and they date back to when a shallow sea covered the area. The rocks in the canyon, including

The Maxwell Trail leads to the refreshing water of West Clear Creek. | NICK BEREZENKO

the behemoth behind you, are sandstone, which also was deposited as sediment in an ancient ocean.

While you're looking at the rocks and smelling the pines, listen for the sounds of birds. Unless the continents happen to collide in the middle of your hike, you're going to hear birds. Lots of birds. The word you'll be looking for is *cacophony*. That's the word Walt Whitman would have used to describe the sound. Of course, he would have also used about 2,000 other words, as well, but cacophony is all you need.

Whatever word(s) you use, at this point, you'll have fully experienced the sights, sounds and smells of the Maxwell Trail. So, now is a good time to bring in the touch. Just beyond the large rock wall are three stately ponderosas. Pat them on the back as you go by, but do it gently, and continue watching your step. What this trail lacks in length it makes up for in adventure. Pay attention, and after another 10 minutes you'll catch the first sounds of the creek. This is the carrot juice at the end of the stick — the highlight of the hike.

In all, it's about 45 minutes from top to bottom — longer on the way out — and along the way you'll go from a transition zone of ponderosas, Douglas firs and Gambel oaks to a riparian zone of red-osier dogwoods, ash, willows and box elders. The trail ends at the creek, which provides habitat for bluegills, chubs and suckers. Dragonflies like the moisture, as

The road to this trail takes you past a former horse ranch known as Poor Farm, which was homesteaded in 1908 by a young man from Kansas named Irvin Henry Walker. Walker and his cowboy cohorts constructed a very basic log cabin next to the pasture where they kept the horses. During a snowstorm, Walker, his partner Norvell Cherry and some fellow cowboys gathered around the cabin's wood stove, trying to stay warm in their sadly constructed shelter. Cherry is said to have told Walker, "If you ask me, this is a damn poor farm." That's allegedly how Poor Farm got its name.

Striated sandstone walls reflect off West Clear Creek near the Maxwell Trail. | NICK BEREZENKO

well. And so will you. The sound of the creek, the sunlight dancing off the water, the grass, the shrubs, the trees surrounded by large rock walls ... that's the climax of the Maxwell Trail. Drink it in, and pack your garbage out. Remember, it takes forever for some of that stuff to biodegrade.

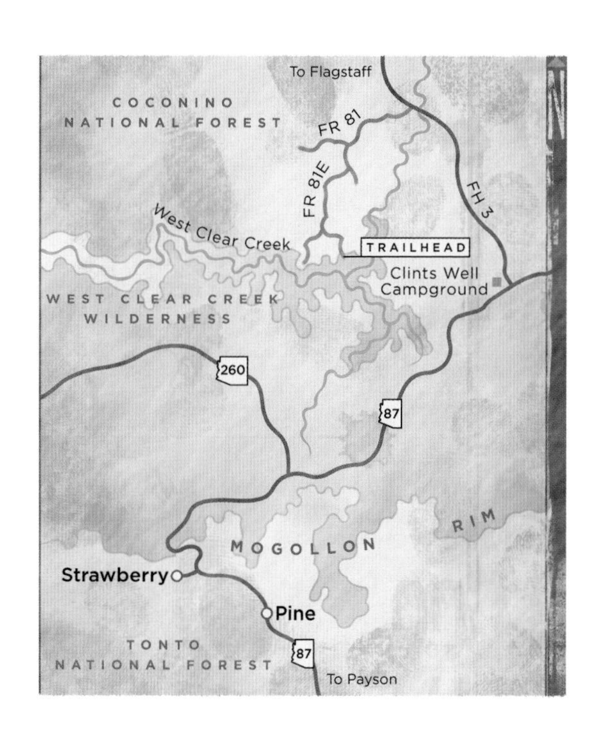

23 | TRAIL GUIDE

Length: 1.4 miles round-trip
Difficulty: Moderate
Elevation: 6,710 to 6,089 feet
Trailhead GPS: N 34°33.345′, W 111°24.295′
Directions: From Clints Well at the junction of State Route 87 and Forest Highway 3 (Lake Mary Road), drive north on FH 3 for approximately 7 miles to Forest Road 81. Turn left onto FR 81 and drive approximately 4 miles to Forest Road 81E. Go left on FR 81E and continue to the end of the road.
Vehicle Requirements: High-clearance required
Dogs Allowed: Yes (on a leash)
USGS Map: Calloway Butte
Information: Mogollon Rim Ranger District, 928-477-2255 or www.fs.fed.us/r3/coconino

Oak Trail

Tonto National Forest | Mogollon Rim

Unlike *For What It's Worth*, the Buffalo Springfield hit that doesn't include the song title in its lyrics, there's an obvious reason for the name of this trail: Oaks are the main attraction, especially toward the end of the hike, where they shade Oak Spring — a refreshing little trickle that helps nourish the canyon of the same name. Indeed, oaks are everywhere. Specifically, Arizona white oaks. The medium-sized evergreens with stout branches rank as some of the largest oaks in the Southwest. They thrive in deep, moist canyons — thus the big boys in Oak Spring Canyon.

In addition to its impressive hardwoods, the Oak Trail is also part of the Arizona Trail, an 819-mile route that runs the length of the state from Utah to Mexico, and was named a National Scenic Trail in 2009. Although it's not the most popular section of the mother trail, the Oak Trail offers a great introduction to the ecosystem below the Mogollon Rim.

The route begins at the Pine Trailhead, a spacious staging area located just south of the little town of Pine. Expect to see horse trailers as well as SUVs in the parking lot. The Arizona Trail, which heads in both directions from this point, is very popular with equestrians.

The Oak Trail is one of many that make up the Arizona Trail. | NICK BEREZENKO

The Arizona white oaks for which this trail is named are most prominent in Oak Spring Canyon. | NICK BEREZENKO

From the parking area, look for the trailhead sign toward the southwest corner of the lot. That's where you'll begin. It's important to note that most of the literature for this hike identifies it as a 5-mile round-tripper, but there's also a half-mile trek from the Pine Trailhead to the Oak Trail's official kickoff point on the west side of State Route 87. It's a nice walk, and it winds for about 15 minutes along Pine Creek in the shade of some large ponderosas.

Use caution when crossing the highway — there's no crosswalk — and look for the sign that reads: "Oak Spring Trail #16." About 10 minutes later, the trail gets wider, similar to an ATV trail, and then heads northwest to a small ranch on private property. The trail veers around the ranch and crosses the creek, which can run heavily in the springtime, depending on the level of snowmelt. From the waterline, the trail climbs gradually out of a small valley toward a revegetation area, which is recovering from a fire

The Oak Trail is part of the Arizona Trail, an 819-mile route that covers the length of the state, from Utah to Mexico. It was first envisioned in 1985 by Dale Shewalter, known as the "Father of the Arizona Trail." According to the *Arizona Daily Sun*, "Shewalter once quit work for a year and put perhaps 60,000 miles on his car in the 1980s to lobby landholding state and federal agencies for their approval [of the trail]." His work paid off. In 2009, the Arizona Trail was designated a National Scenic Trail, which at the time was only the ninth in the country.

that burned several years ago. Although you can still see the trail that cuts through the burn area, veer left onto an alternate trail that leads down to a small wetland sprinkled with interesting boulders.

You'll cross some of the rocks, and maybe a few fallen trees, before topping out again at Bradshaw Tank, which is surrounded by young pines and junipers. As you'll see, the fire took out a lot of trees, making the area open and sunny. Unless it's cloudy, of course.

About an hour into the hike, the forest starts to thicken and the oaks start appearing. In addition to the oaks, take note of the views over your left shoulder. If it's been a wet winter, you should see snow on the high ridges across The Narrows, a nearby canyon carved by Pine Creek.

From this point, the trail begins its general descent toward Oak Spring Canyon. The vegetation is thicker and includes some hearty agaves. Also, the views to the southeast are even better than they were before. What you'll notice most, however, are the downhill switchbacks. Although they're not as steep as those on the Grandview Trail (see page 98), you will feel the burn as the trail drops nearly 700 feet to the canyon's floor.

Chances are, there won't be water in the canyon, but you will see the riparian effects of the nearby spring. You'll also see the intersection with the Walnut Trail. When you get there, turn left and continue about 200 yards to a sign for Oak Spring. The spring itself is another 200 feet down the hill. Like most springs, this one doesn't make a lot of noise, but it's quietly impressive, serving as a lifeline to some massive Arizona white oaks. Looking around, it's easy to see how this trail got its name. The trees are impressive. Also, for what it's worth, there's a gorgeous meadow nearby. It's the perfect place to chill out, grab a snack and admire the oaks.

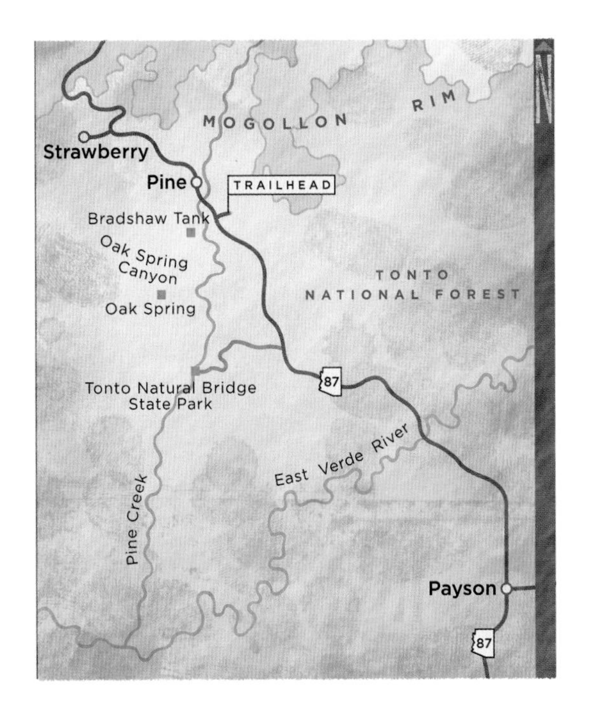

24 | TRAIL GUIDE

Length: 6 miles round-trip
Difficulty: Moderate
Elevation: 5,417 to 5,074 feet
Trailhead GPS: N 34°22.445', W 111°26.606'
Directions: From Payson, drive north on State Route 87 for 15 miles to the Pine Trailhead, which is on the east side of the highway.
Vehicle Requirements: None; accessible by all vehicles
Dogs Allowed: Yes (on a leash)
USGS Maps: Pine, Buckhead Mesa
Information: Payson Ranger District, 928-474-7900 or www.fs.fed.us/r3/tonto

Oaks & Willows Trail

Juniper Mesa Wilderness | Prescott National Forest

This is the best hike you've never heard of. People in Prescott are probably familiar with it, but the rest of the population ... probably not. There's a reason for that. The Oaks & Willows Trail is located in the remote Juniper Mesa Wilderness Area, which sits in the northern part of the Prescott National Forest. Ironically, despite the trail's secluded nature, it's relatively easy to get to. And the drive that takes you there is one of the most scenic in Central Arizona.

Although Williamson Valley Road, which turns into Forest Road 6, is picturesque and accessible by all vehicles, the trailhead directions found in some literature can be a little confusing. If you're not paying attention, you'll end up making wrong turns left and right. The problem is with the signage. For example, the Forest Service directions instruct you to "turn west on Forest Road 95." However, there's not a sign to indicate that you're actually at Forest Road 95. Instead, there's a sign for County Road 125. The roads are one in the same, but you'd

The Oaks & Willows Trail takes hikers into the remote Juniper Mesa Wilderness. | NICK BEREZENKO

never know that. If you follow the directions in our *Trail Guide* below, you'll be fine.

The scenic trail begins at the north fork of Walnut Creek. Just before you get to the creek you'll pass an enormous alligator juniper. The vegetation in this wilderness area varies according to exposure. On the southern slopes you'll find mostly piñon pines and Utah junipers, while the northern slopes feature alligator junipers and ponderosa pines. And, of course, the wilderness is home to a variety of oaks.

A claret cup cactus blooms in George Wood Canyon along the Oaks & Willows Trail. | NICK BEREZENKO

Once you cross the creek, veer right and scale the small embankment. A few minutes later you'll come to an intersection with the Bull Springs Trail, from which you can see Aztec Peak, an important early pioneer route. From there, the well-maintained trail climbs gradually onto a small mesa. As the name implies, the Juniper Mesa Wilderness is essentially a broad, flat, juniper-clad mesa; however, most of the Oaks & Willows Trail keeps to the woods.

About 20 minutes into the hike, the trail leaves the small mesa — not to be confused with Juniper Mesa, which is yet to come — and drops down into George Wood Canyon. After crossing a small creek, the trail passes a

The Juniper Mesa Wilderness was designated by Congress in 1984 and comprises 7,406 acres. The views from the mesa top include all of Apache Creek Wilderness, and portions of the Granite Mountain, Woodchute and Sycamore Canyon wilderness areas. That much is clear. Less certain is the meaning behind the name of the Oaks & Willows Trail. Although the name *seems* to reflect the trail's flora, you won't actually see any willows along it. The former Oaks & Willows Camp, which was west of the present-day wilderness area, probably lent its name to this trail — part of the camp's old cattle trail parallels today's footpath.

pair of ancient alligator juniper twins. There will be others, along with some hefty ponderosa pines, followed by a nice grove of oaks. Just beyond the oaks, the trail merges into a creekbed and begins a series of steep but moderate switchbacks. This is where most of the elevation gain occurs. The last switch marks your arrival on Juniper Mesa. From there, the trail winds through an open forest of mostly evergreens. There are a few places on the mesa where the trail is hard to follow, but there's a nice contingent of cairns to point you in the right direction.

Continuing across the mesa, the route passes an intersection with the Happy Camp Trail, and a little farther on, an intersection with the Juniper Mesa Trail, which heads eastward into the wilderness area. Along this stretch, the Oaks & Willows Trail follows an old fence line — the wire is mostly gone, but many of the old fence posts (dead trees) remain. In terms of elevation, the Juniper Mesa intersection marks the high point of the hike. Normally, when you hit the apex, your work is done. But not on this trail. From the intersection, the trail parallels Pine Creek and heads downhill for a little more than 2 miles, losing about 800 feet in elevation. Of course, those are feet you'll have to reclaim on your way back out. In the end, instead of climbing about 1,000 feet as the *Trail Guide* suggests, you're actually climbing almost double that.

It's worth it, though, especially when you're sitting at Pine Spring, which marks the end of the trail. It's a lush area dominated by ponderosas and oaks. Like the trail itself and the surrounding wilderness, you've probably never heard of Pine Spring. But once you've seen it, you'll never forget it.

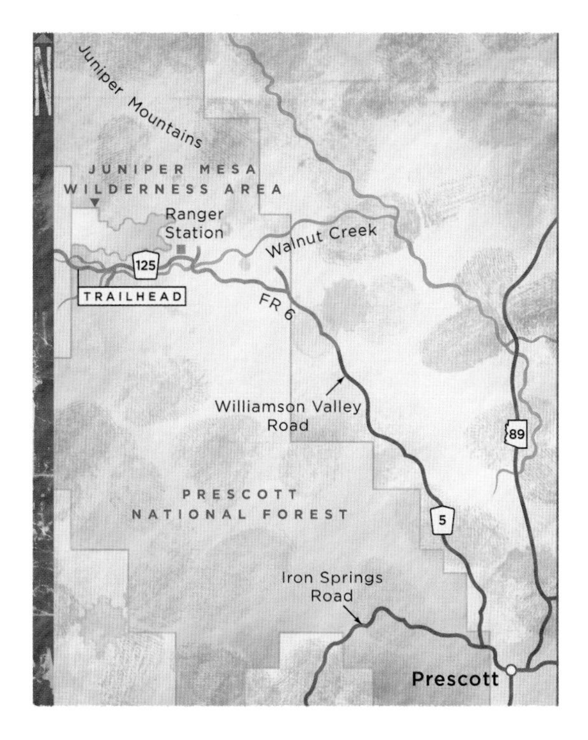

25 | TRAIL GUIDE

Length: 11.5 miles round-trip
Difficulty: Moderate
Elevation: 6,019 to 7,065 feet
Trailhead GPS: N 34°56.455', W 112°57.119'
Directions: From Prescott, drive north on Williamson Valley Road for 22 miles, at which point the pavement ends and the road becomes Forest Road 6. Continue north on FR 6 for 14 miles to the junction with County Road 125 (Forest Road 95). Turn left onto CR 125 and continue for 1.5 miles to the Walnut Creek Ranger Station. From there, continue west on Forest Road 150 for 3.7 miles to a fork in the road, veer right, and continue on FR 150 for 2.8 miles to the trailhead.
Vehicle Requirements: None; accessible by all vehicles
Dogs Allowed: Yes (on a leash)
USGS Map: Juniper Mountains
Information: Chino Ranger District, 928-777-2200 or www.fs.fed.us/r3/prescott

Second Water Trail

Superstition Wilderness | Tonto National Forest

Most trails have a hook — a highlight, a focal point, a reason people hit the trail in the first place. On the Bright Angel, it's the Grand Canyon. On the Weatherford, it's the Inner Basin. And on West Clear Creek, it's West Clear Creek. Throughout most of the year, the centerpiece of any hike in the Superstition Wilderness is the rugged Sonoran Desert landscape — despite its proximity to the fifth-largest city in the United States, this is one of the most remote areas in all of Arizona. In the springtime, however, the hyacinths, anemones, Mexican goldpoppies and desert lupines take center stage.

Nothing against the bluebonnets in Texas or the cherry blossoms in Washington, D.C., but there aren't many wildflower spectacles that can rival the explosion of color that washes over the Arizona desert in February, March and April. To see a delicate flower emerge from the unforgiving soil is a good reminder that Mother Nature is capable of just about anything. It's a sight worth seeing, and there are a number of trails that'll get you there. Second Water is one of the many.

The route begins at the First Water Trailhead. Initially, you'll be on the Dutchman Trail, which leads to Second Water after about 10 minutes. Just beyond the intersection you'll come to First Water Creek. Most of the time, there won't be any water, but in the springtime, it's a possibility. If the water is flowing, you won't need a boat to get across — just a little agility.

A springtime hike in the Superstition Wilderness almost always means a trip through an explosion of desert wildflowers. | PAUL GILL

Garden Valley Arch overlooks Weavers Needle on the Second Water Trail. | PAUL GILL

From there, the clearly marked trail follows a gentle route through saguaros, chollas, paloverdes and ocotillos to an intersection with the Black Mesa Trail. Keep left and look around. After a wet winter, the desert floor in this area, known as Garden Valley, is carpeted with wildflowers and grasses. Think focal point.

Continuing on, there's a steady dose of Sonoran Desert, and after about an hour, you'll come to one of the more interesting saguaros in the world. At some point in its long life, the stately plant suffered some kind of

The legendary Lost Dutchman Gold Mine is allegedly located somewhere in the Superstition Mountains. The mine is named after German immigrant Jacob Waltz. In the late 1800s, "Dutchman" was a common, but thoroughly inaccurate, slang term for "German" — it was derived from the German word for "German," which is "Deutsch." The Lost Dutchman's gold ranks as one of the most famous lost treasures in American history, which is why treasure hunters have been looking for it since at least 1892.

trauma that bent it in half, leaving a good portion of the cactus lying on the ground. Fortunately, the saguaro bent but didn't break, thus allowing it to keep living and keep growing. As of this writing, three new "arms" had sprouted up from the horizontal section on the ground. Like the surrounding wildflowers, this is another one of Mother Nature's many miracles.

Ten minutes beyond the cactus phenomenon, the trail begins a downhill run toward Boulder Canyon. This is where most of the elevation change occurs along the trail. It's not much of a challenge, but it helps deter the masses nonetheless. As you work your way down, you'll see a canyon to your right. That's Second Water Canyon, which parallels Boulder Canyon up ahead. Canyons are common in this wilderness, and they tend to look the same to an untrained eye. It's one of the reasons so many people get lost and, in some cases, die in the Superstitions. There's no risk of getting lost on this trail, though. It's easy to follow and eventually leads to a thicket of reeds growing in a riparian area just before Boulder Canyon. The lush scene will surprise you. And so will the creek that marks the end of the trail.

After about an hour-and-a-half of hiking, you'll come to the intersection with the Boulder Canyon Trail and a tributary of La Barge Creek. Like First Water Creek earlier, there's a good chance of seeing water in this stream if winter storms have delivered an average amount of precipitation. As far as turnaround points on a trail go, this has to rank as one of the most spectacular. The surrounding rock walls of the canyon, the saguaros dotting the landscape, the flowing stream ... it's almost enough to make you forget that wildflowers are the focal point of this hike.

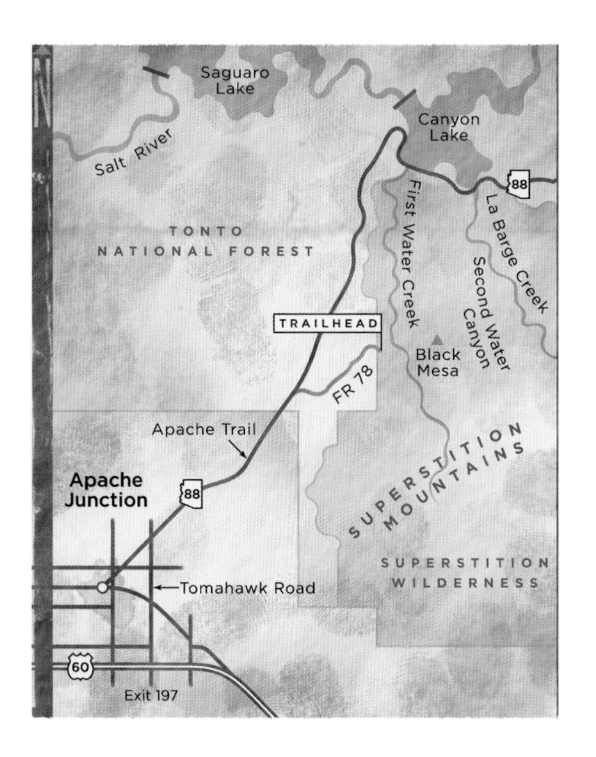

26 | TRAIL GUIDE

Length: 6.6 miles round-trip
Difficulty: Easy
Elevation: 1,940 to 2,420 feet
Trailhead GPS: N 33°28.802', W 111°26.586'
Directions: From Phoenix, drive east on U.S. Route 60 for approximately 25 miles to Tomahawk Road (Exit 197) and turn left. Drive north for 3 miles to State Route 88 (The Apache Trail), turn right and drive approximately 5 miles to the First Water Trailhead, which serves as the starting point for the Second Water Trail, as well.
Vehicle Requirements: None; accessible by all vehicles
Dogs Allowed: Yes (on a leash)
USGS Map: Goldfield
Information: Tonto Ranger District, 928-402-6200 or www.fs.fed.us/r3/tonto

Morning dew glistens on a Hill's lupine on the North Rim of Grand Canyon National Park (see Uncle Jim Trail, page 168, and Widforss Trail, page 176). | NICK BEREZENKO

SUMMER

Bear Creek Trail

Apache-Sitgreaves National Forests | Hannagan Meadow

The idea that "life is a journey, not a destination" is often attributed to Ralph Waldo Emerson. No one knows for sure if it was the great American poet who first combined those seven words, but if it were Emerson, he wasn't referring to the Bear Creek Trail in Eastern Arizona. Nevertheless, it fits the bill.

Although the trail itself is scenic and spectacular — any trail that features the Black River is going to score *a lot* of points — the drive to it is equally impressive. The trip begins at Hannagan Meadow and follows a series of picturesque forest roads to the trailhead. Like most road trips in the White Mountains, this one winds through a lush alpine forest that's interspersed with meadows and streams and herds of elk. Because the roads are dirt and gravel, you can't drive too fast. That's to your benefit — the slower pace turns this back road into a Sunday drive. Enjoy the journey, and then get serious about the destination.

Of all the Easy hikes in this book, this one is one of the easiest. There's a slight elevation change, but it's barely noticeable, and the entire hike is only 1.5 miles round-trip. It's easy, but it's worth exploring — what the Bear Creek Trail lacks in aerobic exercise, it more than makes up for in Mother Nature.

The hike begins at a spacious trailhead near an old corral. Within a few minutes, you'll start hearing the creek for which the trail is named. You won't see it initially, because the creek is overgrown with trees and grasses, but you'll know it's there by the sound it makes.

The Black River flows toward its confluence with Bear Creek in the White Mountains. | NICK BEREZENKO

A red cinquefoil snaps to attention along the Bear Creek Trail. | NICK BEREZENKO

Heading downhill, the trail parallels the creek and evolves from a path of scattered rocks to a path of mostly dirt. Looking around, you'll see that the bulk of the forest is made up of tall ponderosas and Douglas firs. As forests go, this one is fairly open, and it's nothing like the thicket that

There are different theories on how the Black River got its name. One of the earliest is attributed to Lieutenant William Emery of the U.S. Army, who, on October 26, 1846, referred to it as the Prieta River. In Spanish, *prieta* means "dark" or "black." The Black River, which is the turnaround point for this hike, is stocked weekly in the summer with rainbow trout. The Black River eventually merges with the White River to form the Salt River.

exists along the nearby Bear Wallow Trail (see page 136).

About 20 minutes into the hike, the trail veers away from the creek, but not so far that you'll be out of earshot. A few minutes later, the trail passes under a strand of barbed wire — a remnant of an old fence — that's at least 7 feet off the ground. Beyond the fence, the Douglas firs become more prominent, and so do the willows growing along the creek.

Before long, the trail rejoins the creek, and even crosses it at one point. As you're hiking near the water, keep in mind that it's important to tread lightly along the stream banks to prevent erosion. If you want to get your feet wet, the river is just ahead. It's about 5 minutes away, and one of the first things you'll notice when you get there — other than the obvious beauty of the Black River — is that it's bordered by a formidable wall of shrubs and grasses. Before you try penetrating the defense, look carefully where you're stepping. Poison ivy is a year-round resident in the White Mountains, and it's especially abundant along many parts of this trail. The river's edge is no exception.

If you look to the right of where the trail meets the river, you'll notice that the path continues for about 100 yards to the east. Head that way and you'll come to an opening in the brush that allows access to the river. You might have to sidestep some poison ivy in the process (remember: "leaves of three, let it be"), but the reward is worth the risk. As you'll see, the Black River is one of the scenic wonders of Eastern Arizona, and it's the highlight of this hike. In fact, it's so impressive that while you're standing there, there's a good chance you'll start questioning Emerson's theory. Maybe it *is* about the destination. Or maybe in some cases, like the Bear Creek Trail, it's about both.

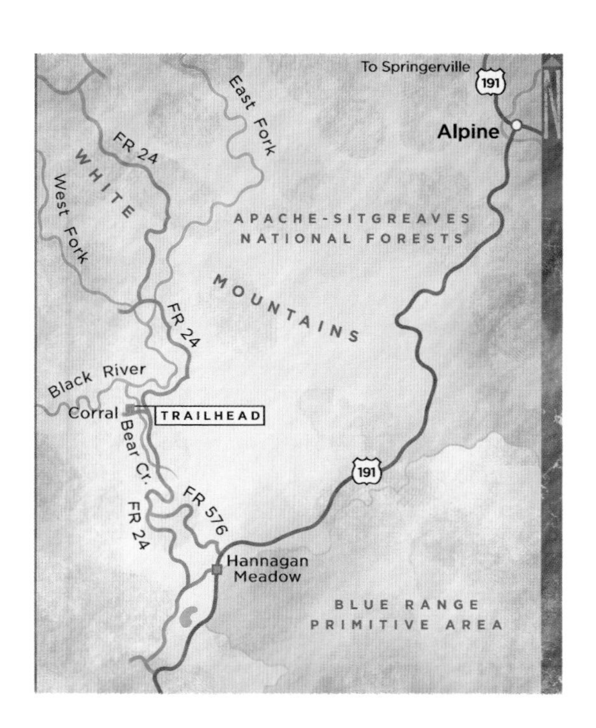

27 | TRAIL GUIDE

Length: 1.5 miles round-trip
Difficulty: Easy
Elevation: 7,428 to 7,139 feet
Trailhead GPS: N 33°42.960', W 109°22.320'
Directions: From Hannagan Meadow, drive west on Forest Road 576 for 4 miles to Forest Road 24. Turn right onto FR 24 and drive 7.3 miles to an old corral on the left. Just past the corral is a dirt road. Turn left onto the dirt road and drive 200 yards to the trailhead.
Vehicle Requirements: None; accessible by all vehicles
Dogs Allowed: Yes (on a leash)
USGS Maps: Hannagan Meadow, Hoodoo Knoll
Information: Alpine Ranger District, 928-339-5000 or www.fs.fed.us/r3/asnf

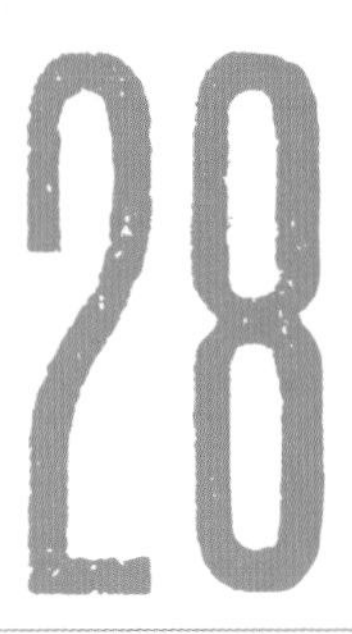

Bear Wallow Trail

Bear Wallow Wilderness | Hannagan Meadow

Bears get top billing on this hike, but don't get your hopes up — you're more likely to see deer, turkeys, squirrels, coyotes and songbirds. And maybe an elk or even a spotted owl. Even so, there *are* bears in the Bear Wallow Wilderness, and your chances of seeing one are better on this trail than they are on the other two "bear" trails in this book: Bear Canyon (see page 28) and Bear Creek (see page 132). In fact, some biologists believe that Bear Wallow and the surrounding backcountry contain the largest concentration of black bears in Arizona. They're out there, but they like to keep their distance.

Whether or not you see bears, you will see their wallows, which are wet, boggy areas where the elusive omnivores like to roll around and rid themselves of parasites and biting insects. For *Ursus americanus*, the wallows serve a practical purpose. For Homo sapiens, they simply add to the scenic beauty of a hike that winds through some of the most remote and wild terrain in the state.

The trail begins with a gradual descent through a forest of just about every alpine species you can imagine: Douglas firs, Engelmann spruce, Colorado blue spruce, quaking aspens. Mature ponderosas elbow in, as well. Arboreal is an adjective that'll come to mind — over and over — on this spectacular hike.

After about 15 minutes, the trail arrives at a small meadow. In the

The dense forest of Bear Wallow Wilderness, in keeping with its name, is home to a large concentration of black bears. | DAVID MUENCH

Flower-filled meadows, called *cienegas*, are common in the White Mountains and offer a good opportunity to see wildlife. | DAVID MUENCH

White Mountains, meadows are called *cienegas*, which is Spanish for "wet, marshy areas." Just beyond the small *cienega* is a massive Douglas fir — one of the largest you'll see all day — and on the breeze you'll hear the sounds of birds. Lots of birds. Especially woodpeckers. Fifteen minutes later, after a half-hour of hiking, the trail reaches the North Fork of Bear Wallow Creek. This year-round waterway, which is lined with evergreens, oaks and box elders, is the centerpiece of the hike, and it's the compass you'll use to get from one end of the wilderness to the other.

Heading downstream, the trail follows the creek and crosses it several times. Most of the crossings are simple, but before the day is done, you *will* get your feet wet. But don't worry about the water. Instead, worry about the poison ivy. The only thing that keeps this trail from being perfect is that three-leafed demon. As much as you'll be tempted to wear shorts on this hike, overcome the urge and wear long pants.

Before long, about an hour into the hike, the Bear Wallow Trail intersects the Reno Trail, which drops down from the ridge to the north. Although most of the wilderness is thick with underbrush, the area around this junction is a little more open, and it offers a good opportunity to see

Just up the road from the Bear Wallow Wilderness is Hannagan Meadow, which is named for Robert Hannagan, a Nevada miner who decided to try his hand at cattle ranching in Eastern Arizona. He came to the area in the late 1890s, and, as the story goes, eventually ended up in debt, owing $1,200 to a couple of brothers. For whatever reason, Hannagan decided not to pay, so the brothers yanked him off an outbound stagecoach and chained him to a tree. Eventually, Hannagan's son wired the money from New Mexico, and the old man was cut loose.

wildlife — if your timing is right. Twenty minutes later you'll come to a second intersection. This time with the Schell Canyon Trail, which is where the north and south forks of Bear Wallow Creek come together. This makes a good turnaround point for anyone looking for a shorter day hike. The Schell Canyon intersection is 3.5 miles from the trailhead.

Continuing on, keep to the right and keep your focus. For the next couple of miles, the trail gets a little tricky to follow, especially at the various creek crossings. It's the thickets that complicate things, and in some cases, you might even have to part the willows with your hands. You won't get lost, but you don't want to get detoured too far, either. Stick close to the creek and you'll be OK.

Eventually, after some minor bushwhacking and multiple creek crossings, you'll come to a small burn area, followed by a fish barrier that was built to protect the creek's threatened population of Apache trout. The barrier is made of caged rocks and is there to keep the more prominent rainbow trout from diluting the genetic stock of the Apache trout. The trail crosses over the barrier and winds for about 15 minutes to an intersection with the Gobbler Point Trail.

The Gobbler goes right while the Bear Wallow continues for a half-mile to the boundary of the San Carlos Apache Reservation, which is marked by an old barbed-wire fence. The fence is hard to find, and there's no official metal sign announcing your arrival at the reservation. Nevertheless, you'll need to know where you are because it's illegal to cross onto the reservation without a permit. Don't press your luck. It's bad enough to hike all day and not see a bear. It would be even worse to go home with a ticket for trespassing.

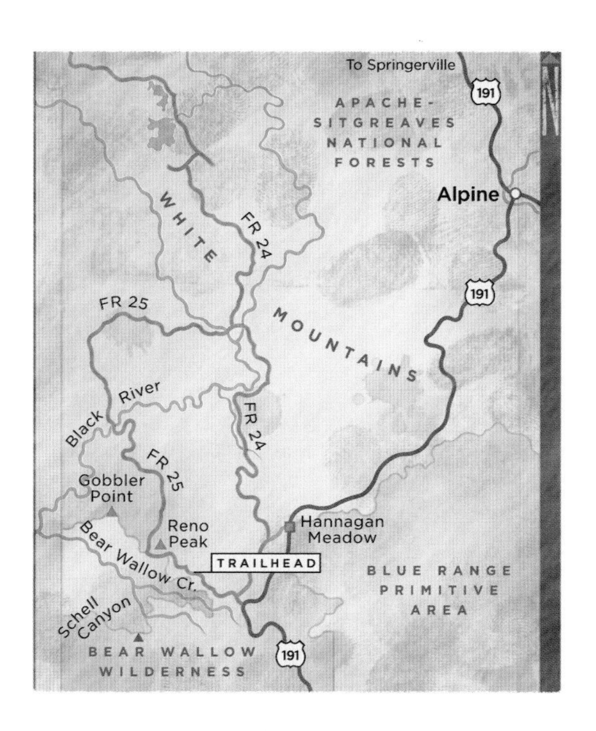

28 | TRAIL GUIDE

Length: 15.2 miles round-trip
Difficulty: Strenuous
Elevation: 8,720 to 6,657 feet
Trailhead GPS: N 33°36.189', W 109°23.849'
Directions: From Hannagan Meadow, drive south on U.S. Route 191 for 5 miles to Forest Road 25. Turn right onto FR 25 and drive 3 miles to the trailhead.
Vehicle Requirements: None; accessible by all vehicles
Dogs Allowed: Yes (on a leash)
USGS Maps: Baldy Bill Point, Hoodoo Knoll
Information: Alpine Ranger District, 928-339-5000 or www.fs.fed.us/r3/asnf

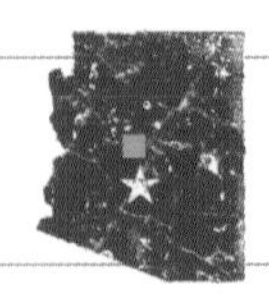

Groom Creek Loop

Prescott National Forest | Prescott

At one time, Prescott was the capital city of Arizona. There are many reasons it was moved to Phoenix. The Groom Creek Loop wasn't among them. This moderate trek is one of Prescott's points of pride. In fact, it's one of the best trails in the Prescott National Forest. Along with a pretty good workout, the loop offers more than its share of scenery, especially from the top of Spruce Mountain, from which you can see Crown King, Prescott and, on a clear day, the San Francisco Peaks.

From the trailhead, the loop, which is marked Trail No. 307, veers left along a soft path — it'll feel like you're walking on sand. For the first few minutes, the trail parallels Forest Road 52, but the road fades away as you begin the 1,200-foot climb toward the top. Moving uphill, beware of downhill mountain-bikers. They tend to fly. Watch for horses, too. Because of its proximity to Prescott, this trail is popular with a wide range of outdoor enthusiasts.

About 15 minutes into the hike, you'll come to a boulder the size of a small Winnebago. Its girth is impressive, and so is the vertical crack that splits it in two. Looking around the rock, you'll notice that the forest isn't as dense as others you might have hiked. That's because it's made up mostly of alligator junipers, oaks and a scattering of ponderosa pines. You'll also see some firs as you get higher up the mountain. What you won't see are spruce trees. The tree for which the summit is named doesn't grow in this forest. What the early settlers thought were spruce trees are actually white firs.

Granite boulders mix with oak chaparral and ponderosa pines along the Groom Creek Loop trail. | NICK BEREZENKO

The Groom Creek Loop leads to the top of Spruce Mountain, which is covered with evergreens. | CHRISTINE KEITH

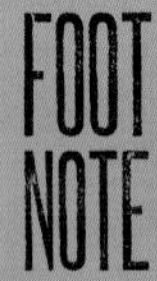

Along this trail, see if you can spot the abandoned crab-apple orchard and the remains of an old mining cabin. They're easy to miss, but a treat when you find them. Another sideshow is the Spruce Mountain lookout tower, which was erected in 1936 and is on the National Historic Lookout Register.

Continuing on, the trail gets rocky and eventually leads to an intersection that can be a little confusing. Follow the arrow for Trail No. 307 and you'll be headed in the right direction. Spruce Mountain is about an hour from this point, and for most of those 60 minutes the terrain remains about the same. At the top of the mountain, you'll see some picnic tables and a fire tower. Although the tower is there year-round, the rangers who occupy it are not. During the fire season, when the tower is in use, hikers are encouraged to climb up and say hello.

The views are great, but the lesson in forest ecology is equally impressive. Among other things, you'll learn that one of the reasons this forest isn't as thick as others is because of bark beetles. In 2002 and 2003, the insects killed approximately 18 million ponderosas in Arizona. A couple years later, as part of a fire-management program, many living trees and most of the beetle-killed trees were removed from this area. The move is expected to reduce the risk of both forest fires and beetle epidemics. Time will tell.

From the picnic tables, the Groom Creek Loop begins its downhill run. One of the first things you'll see is an alligator juniper that's at least 6 feet in diameter. Pose for a photo, and then follow the trail through the forest of ponderosas and firs to where it intersects the Isabella Trail. There will be other intersections, too, and most are adequately marked, but some are not. Don't head off in any direction until you know for sure where you're going.

The rest of the route winds down the mountain, through a small ravine, and back to the trailhead. Standing there, in the shade of the tall pines, it's hard to imagine that downtown Prescott is just a few miles away. In a city with a long list of points of pride, Trail No. 307 just might be "No. 1."

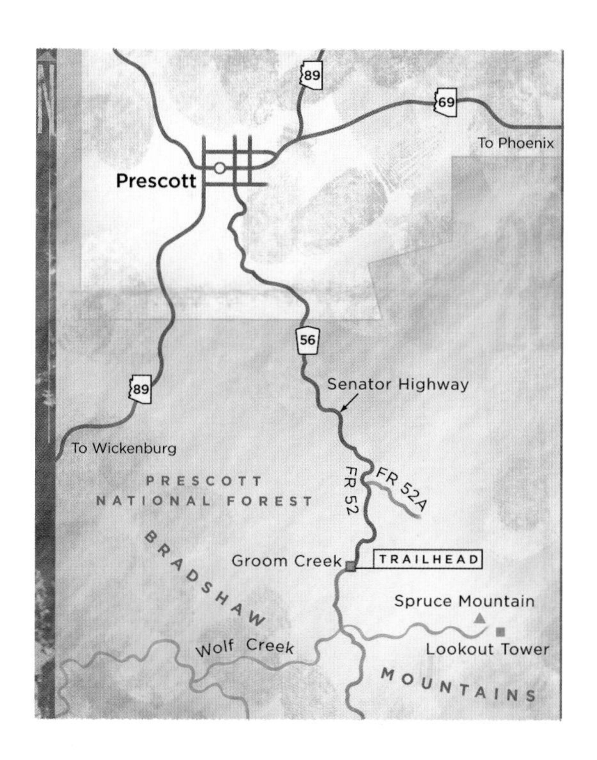

29 | TRAIL GUIDE

Length: 8.7-mile loop
Difficulty: Moderate
Elevation: 6,400 to 7,693 feet
Trailhead GPS: N 34°28.134', W 112°26.280'
Directions: From Prescott, take Gurley Street east to Mt. Vernon Avenue (Senator Highway, Forest Road 52), turn right and drive approximately 6.4 miles to the trailhead, which is on the left side of the road.
Vehicle Requirements: None; accessible by all vehicles
Dogs Allowed: Yes (on a leash)
USGS Map: Groom Creek
Information: Bradshaw Ranger District, 928-443-8000 or www.fs.fed.us/r3/prescott

Horton Creek Trail

Tonto National Forest | Mogollon Rim

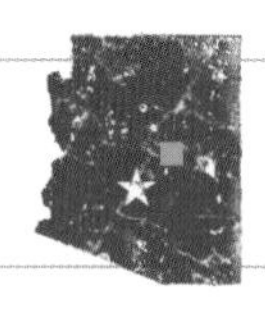

Horton was an elephant who heard a Who. He was born in the imagination of Dr. Seuss, and was later "voiced" by Jim Carrey in an animated film. Horton Creek has nothing to do with any of that, and no matter how hard you listen, you won't hear a Who along this trail. You will, however, hear water, which in Arizona is always like music to the ears.

The trail, which is named for the creek that's named for settler L.J. Horton, begins at the foot of the Mogollon Rim, about 150 feet from the Upper Tonto Creek Campground, and follows an old logging road that parallels the stream. The first quarter-mile or so is an easy pine-needle-covered path that cuts through a grove of ponderosas and aspens. To this point, you won't hear any water, but once you pass the Forest Service gate, you'll start hearing the creek.

For most of the hike, you'll be within a few hundred yards of the water. By all means, hop off the trail and get your feet wet. There are several creek-crossings — made up of big rocks and small boulders, which are slippery when wet — and they're worth the side trip. You'll also notice some idyllic campsites, which you'll want to keep in mind for another day.

Continuing uphill, past the lush colonies of roses, wild grapes, ferns and strawberries, you might start feeling a burn in your quads. It's not poison ivy, although that diabolical plant does grow in the area. The burn is from the incline, which is unexpected — this hike is deceptively steep,

Horton Creek cascades over mossy rocks as it makes its way from Horton Spring to Tonto Creek. | NICK BEREZENKO

Horton Spring originates at the base of Horseshoe Lake Point on the Mogollon Rim. | NICK BEREZENKO

and gains more than 1,000 feet in elevation. Another challenge, as you get farther up, is a bed of rocks created by an old rockslide. Be careful — the trail winds over the rocks, which drool at the thought of twisting unsuspecting ankles.

Eventually, you'll leave the rocky stretch and, at the 1.5-mile mark, you'll see a monstrous alligator juniper to your left — this tree is to junipers what the General Sherman is to giant sequoias. The surrounding maples and Douglas firs are impressive, as well. Everywhere you look, the views are worth a thousand words.

The nature of the trail stays about the same until it nears the top,

Located just 3 miles east of this trail is the place where Zane Grey's cabin once stood. The cabin, which was built in the 1920s and destroyed by the Dude Fire in 1990, was a historic landmark of sorts. The acclaimed author of *Riders of the Purple Sage* and other famous Western novels penned many of his classics at the cabin. Today, a replica cabin is open for tours in nearby Payson.

where a series of switchbacks lead away from the creek. Don't be fooled by that. At the 4-mile mark, the Horton Creek Trail intersects the Highline Trail, which is a 40-mile marathon for those lucky hikers who don't have to be at work on Monday morning.

Pine cones are common on the Mogollon Rim, which is home to the largest ponderosa pine forest in the world. | RANDY PRENTICE

Just beyond that intersection is Horton Spring, which pours out of the rocks about 30 feet above the stream and nurtures the lush surroundings made up of horsetails, mosses and grasses. These are the headwaters of the creek, and if ever there were a place to relax and get lost in your imagination, this would be it. You won't hear a Who, but who cares?

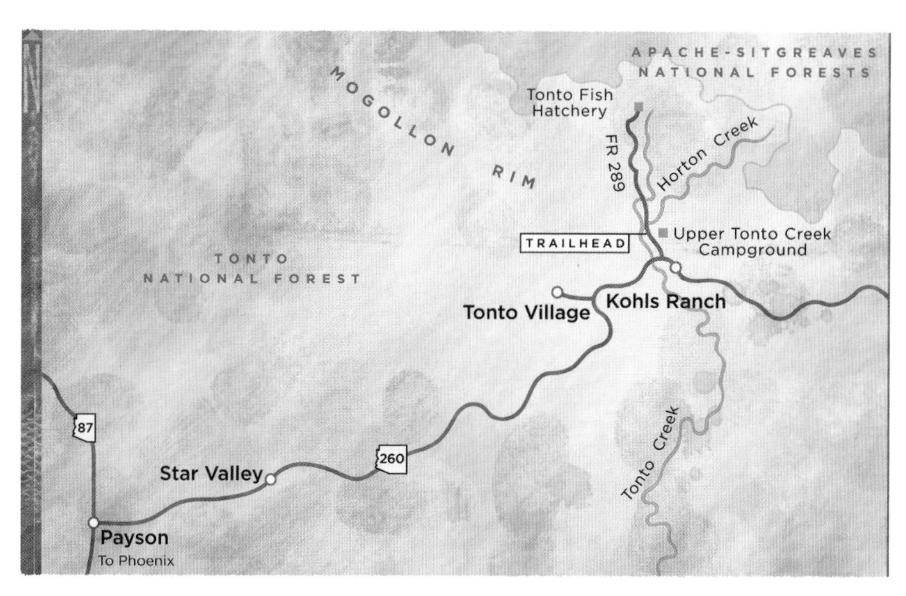

30 TRAIL GUIDE

Length: 8 miles round-trip
Difficulty: Moderate
Elevation: 5,360 to 6,700 feet
Trailhead GPS: N 34°20.394', W 111°05.732'
Directions: From Payson, drive east on State Route 260 for 17 miles to Tonto Creek Road (Forest Road 289) near Kohls Ranch, turn left and drive 1 mile to the Upper Tonto Creek Campground. The trailhead is at the campground.
Vehicle Requirements: None; accessible by all vehicles
Dogs Allowed: Yes (on a leash)
USGS Map: Promontory Butte
Information: Black Mesa Ranger District, 928-535-7300 or www.fs.fed.us/r3/tonto

Humphreys Peak Trail
Kachina Peaks Wilderness | Flagstaff

Humphreys Peak is the king of the hills in Arizona. It's the pinnacle. The highest point in the state. If you can make it to the summit, which tops out at 12,633 feet, you've conquered all there is to conquer — from a hiking perspective, anyway. Making it up and down is certainly something to be proud of, but, despite its stature, the Hump is not the most difficult hike in Arizona. The North Kaibab Trail (see page 210), from river to rim, is more challenging. And so are others. Still, this one ranks right up there.

The trail begins at the far end of the lower parking lot for Arizona Snowbowl Ski Resort. After a short climb through a lush meadow of grasses and wildflowers, you'll start to smell the evergreens as the trail enters the deep forest. About the time the sky disappears, you'll be crossing into the Kachina Peaks Wilderness Area. Humphreys Peak, along with three others — Agassiz (12,365 feet), Fremont (11,969 feet) and Doyle (11,460 feet) — comprise the Kachina Peaks, which are sacred to the Navajo, Hopi, Havasupai and Zuni peoples. Many, many years ago, the peaks were part of a single volcano, and the Inner Basin was its crater.

Although reaching the summit is the high point of this hike, there's a lot to see in the process, including thousands of acres of Engelmann spruce, corkbark fir, ponderosa pines and even some aspens. Wildlife is plentiful, too. Look for Western bluebirds, chickadees, white-throated swifts, wild turkeys, porcupines, mountain lions, bobcats, elk, black bears

Columbines grow among the aspens and evergreens along the Humphreys Peak Trail north of Flagstaff. | TOM BROWNOLD

The Humphreys Peak Trail takes hikers to Arizona's only tundra region. | TOM BEAN

and mule deer. The most common animal, however, is the human being. This is a popular trail, but because of the elevation gain and the lack of oxygen higher up, hikers tend to thin out.

From the edge of the forest, the well-maintained trail climbs for several miles to the Agassiz Saddle, which connects Humphreys and Agassiz peaks. This is also where the Humphreys Trail intersects the Weatherford Trail (see page 230). You'll be heading uphill, but look around.

Humphreys Peak was named in 1870 for General Andrew A. Humphreys, a Union general during the American Civil War. In 1911, when a General Land Office map from 1903 showed the name "San Francisco Peak" applied to what is now Humphreys Peak, the United States Board on Geographic Names approved the variant name. However, in 1933, the application was rectified and Humphreys Peak once again became Humphreys Peak.

Up to this point, most of the hike has been a tunnel through the thick alpine forest. The saddle affords an opportunity to see what you've been missing, including the devastating effects of the Schultz Fire, which burned 15,000 acres in June 2010. Of course, the views from the top go on forever.

Before you get there, though, you'll notice that the tree line has thinned out. The saddle marks the beginning of Arizona's only tundra region. At that level, nothing but bristlecone pines can survive, and even those disappear before the peak. Like all tundra regions, this one is extremely fragile, which is why the Forest Service strictly prohibits camping and off-trail hiking. Perhaps more than anything, the goal is to protect the San Francisco Peaks groundsel (*Senecio franciscanus*), an extremely rare plant that grows nowhere else in the world.

Watch your step and gear up for the last mile or so to the summit. It's the most challenging stretch of the hike. It's worth the effort, though. At 12,633 feet, you'll be able to see the Grand Canyon and the Hopi mesas to the north, the White Mountains to the east and Oak Creek Canyon to the south. And, overhead, you might see some of those white-throated swifts feeding on the insects that'll be swarming around your face. Your biggest concern, however, won't be the bugs, but rather the weather.

Around the peaks, thunderstorms and their deadly lightning strikes can roll in almost without warning. Don't press your luck, and remember the first rule of mountain-climbing: Making it down is more important than making it up. After all, there's no point in conquering the king of the hills if you're not going to be around to brag about it.

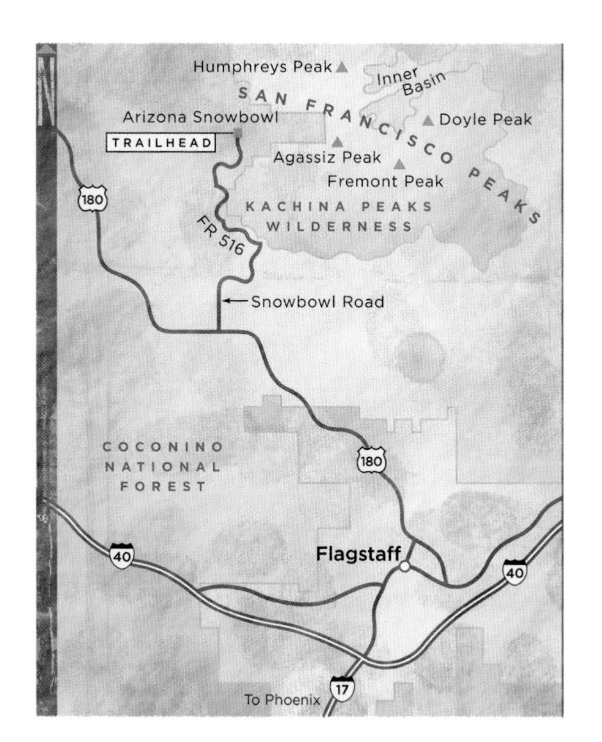

31 | TRAIL GUIDE

Length: 9 miles round-trip
Difficulty: Strenuous
Elevation: 9,327 to 12,633 feet
Trailhead GPS: N 35°19.881', W 111°42.694'
Directions: From Flagstaff, drive north on U.S. Route 180 for 7 miles to Forest Road 516 (Snowbowl Road), turn right and continue another 6.3 miles to the lower parking lot. The trailhead is at the far end of the lot.
Vehicle Requirements: None; accessible by all vehicles
Dogs Allowed: Yes (on a leash)
USGS Map: Humphreys Peak
Information: Peaks Ranger District, 928-526-0866 or www.fs.fed.us/r3/coconino

32

Marshall Lake to Fisher Point Trail

Arizona Trail | Coconino National Forest

One thousand, nine hundred and thirteen. That's how many miles separate Flagstaff, Arizona, and Washington, D.C. With that kind of distance, and all of the other priorities of the president, few people would have expected Barack Obama to make time for the Arizona Trail. But on March 30, 2009, he signed House Resolution 146, which, among other things, added the 819-mile trail to the exclusive list of National Scenic Trails.

Prior to the president's signature, there were just eight National Scenic Trails in the country. Now, the Arizona Trail is among an elite group that includes the Pacific Crest Trail, the Ice Age Trail and the Appalachian Trail. Beyond the prestige, the designation is significant because it provides a new level of

The San Francisco Peaks reflect in Marshall Lake, which is the starting point for one of the easiest segments of the Arizona Trail. | TOM BEAN

Ponderosa pines dominate the Coconino National Forest. | TOM BEAN

protection for the state's ultimate hike.

One of the easiest and most accessible sections of the Arizona Trail, which runs the length of the state from Mexico to Utah, is the route from Marshall Lake to Fisher Point near Flagstaff. Named for the guy who incorporated the first bank in Flagstaff, Marshall Lake is more marsh than lake. Still, it's a vital wetland that provides habitat for an array of birds, including osprey and bald eagles. What's more, it's beautiful.

From the lake, the easy-to-follow trail (think cow path) cuts across Anderson Mesa, a broad, grassy upland dotted with trees. After about 20 minutes, the trail drops into a ponderosa forest. Although you'll be surrounded by trees, it's nothing compared to the smothering effect of the Appalachian Trail, which, according to Bill Bryson, can be overwhelming. As he wrote in *A Walk in the Woods*, his excellent book about hiking the country's oldest National Scenic Trail: "Woods are not like other spaces. Their trees surround you, loom over you, press in from all sides. Woods choke off views and leave you muddled and without bearings."

Fisher Point is the highest point of this hike. The rock wall that supports the point is made up of limestone, which means Fisher Point was once at the bottom of an inland sea/lake. If you look closely, fossils can be seen in the rock. The Pit, a well-known rock-climbing area, is located nearby — where the trail drops down into Walnut Canyon.

The route from Marshall Lake is nothing like that. In fact, it's so open there's a good chance you'll see some wildlife. Keep your eyes peeled for elk, mule deer, turkeys and coyotes. Continuing downhill for another 10 or 15 minutes, you'll arrive at a small meadow, which gives way to more trees and a brief uphill climb. The trail continues like this for about an hour, after which you'll come to the ridgeline of Walnut Canyon. Whether you're ready or not, you'll want to take a break at this spot. The views of the San Francisco Peaks are spectacular — maybe as good as you'll get anywhere.

Moving on, the trail switchbacks to the bottom of the canyon — the same canyon that includes Walnut Canyon National Monument — and passes some beautiful red-rock cliffs reminiscent of Sedona, but with a hint of pink, as well. Eventually, you'll wind up in a large open meadow with a couple of trails going in different directions. Follow the signs to Fisher Point. You could turn around at the meadow, but the extra 1.1 miles (one way) to the point are worth the effort. From the top, you can see distant horizons and the meadow you crossed below. And like any apex, it's a perfect place to reflect on the first half of the hike. It's also a good opportunity to look toward Washington and be grateful for HR 146.

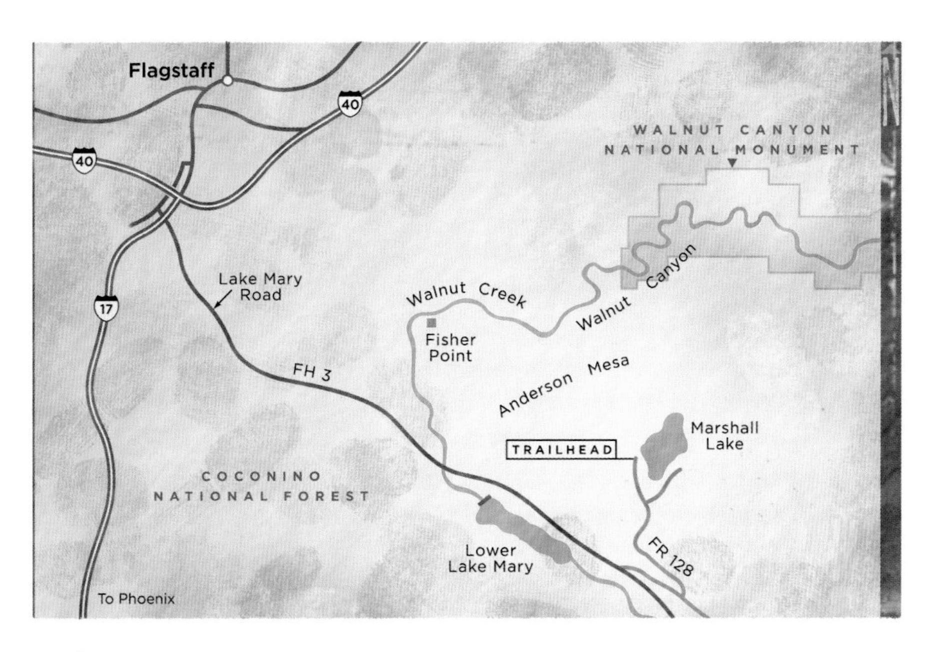

Length: 13.6 miles round-trip
Difficulty: Moderate
Elevation: 7,137 to 7,708 feet
Trailhead GPS: N 35°06.672', W 111°32.487'
Directions: From Flagstaff, drive southeast on Forest Highway 3 (Lake Mary Road) for 9.5 miles to Forest Road 128. Turn left onto FR 128 and continue 1.2 miles to a fork in the road. Turn left at the fork and drive a half-mile to an intersection with an unmarked dirt road (look for the Forest Service sign marking Marshall Lake). Turn left onto the dirt road and drive a quarter-mile to the trailhead.
Vehicle Requirements: None; accessible by all vehicles
Dogs Allowed: Yes (on a leash)
USGS Maps: Flagstaff East, Lower Lake Mary
Information: Peaks/Mormon Lakes Ranger Districts, 928-526-0866 or www.fs.fed.us/r3/coconino

33

Mormon Mountain Trail

Coconino National Forest | Mormon Lake

Ponderosa pines can get old. Not in the figurative sense of, "Eh, if I see one more ponderosa I'm going to scream," but literally old. Some can live anywhere from 200 to 500 years. Compared to the redwoods, that's nothing, but in Northern Arizona, it's impressive. That's why old-growth forests like the one surrounding the Mormon Mountain Trail are so special.

Like all old and well-established forests, this one is made up of big trees, snags (large, standing dead trees), downed logs, clumps of younger trees, seedlings and small clearings. The snags in particular are vital to the survival of the forest because they provide habitat for birds and other small creatures, which then become food for the resident hawks, eagles, bears, coyotes and foxes. It's all part of a sophisticated ecosystem, and you'll get a firsthand look on this hike.

The San Francisco Peaks can be seen from the Mormon Mountain Trail, which winds through an old-growth forest in Northern Arizona. | TOM BEAN

Mule deer, along with bears and coyotes, can be seen on the Mormon Mountain Trail. | TOM BEAN

The quiet trail begins at the far end of Dairy Springs Campground. For the first few minutes, it overlaps a self-guided nature trail in the campground. Before long, though, you'll come to a gate, beyond which is an intersection with the Arizona Trail. In case you're wondering, it's 28.4 miles from this point to Flagstaff, and the Arizona Trail as a whole is 819 miles from Mexico to Utah. But you're not taking the Arizona Trail. Not now, anyway. Instead, you're going straight.

After about 15 or 20 minutes, the forest of mixed conifers and oaks opens up briefly, offering your first glimpse of Mormon Lake, as well as the

Between 1876 and 1878, Mormon settlers established a dairy not far from this trailhead. Beginning with a herd of 115 cows, the dairy produced large quantities of butter and cheese that were delivered to various towns around the state. The dairy closed in 1886.

grassy flats and forest-covered hills that surround it. Depending on the time of year, and what the weather's been like, the lake may or may not have water in it. Either way, you'll get your bearings. You'll also see signs of the elk that use this trail to get wherever it is they're going. Yet another highlight as you move along is the abundance of wildflowers, especially in June. Initially, you'll see a few flowers springing up among the trees, but when you hit the 60-minute mark of the hike, you'll come to a small grassy meadow that's often flooded with lupines and other flowers.

Just beyond the meadow, the first aspen appears off to the right. There are a few others along the way, but this is primarily a ponderosa forest. By the way, you can tell the age of a ponderosa by its bark. For the first 120 to 150 years of its life, its bark is blackish. As it gets older, the bark changes to a yellowish-red color and forms the flat "plates" you're familiar with. That's where the nickname "yellow belly" comes from.

The trail stays much the same for the next half-hour, climbing gradually through the pines and occasional aspens. Then, after about an hour-and-a-half, the underbrush thickens with grasses and shrubs. This is your best bet for seeing an elk. Heed the advice of Elmer Fudd and you might get lucky. If not, you will see butterflies. They're everywhere.

From there, it's a quick scamper to a large meadow that marks the end of the trail. At this point, you can either turn around and head back or follow Forest Road 648 to the 8,449-foot summit of Mormon Mountain. If you have the energy, you might as well go to the top. Among other things, it'll give you a little more time to appreciate the special nature of this old-growth forest.

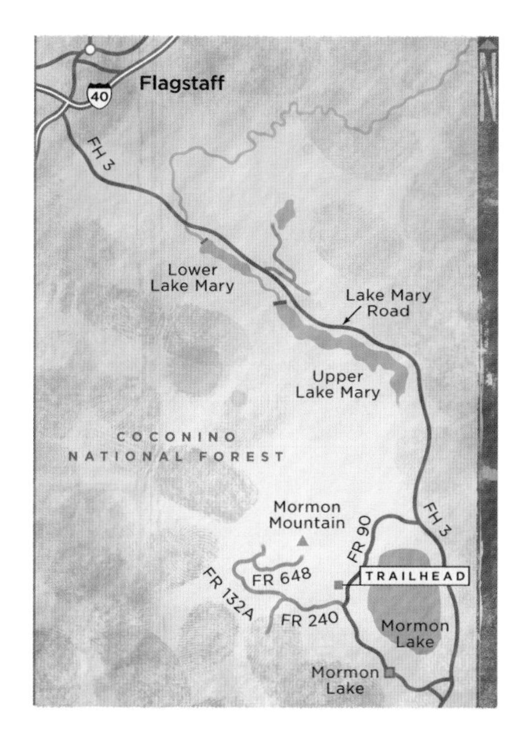

33 | TRAIL GUIDE

Length: 6 miles round-trip
Difficulty: Moderate
Elevation: 7,233 to 8,449 feet
Trailhead GPS: N 34°57.289', W 111°29.268'
Directions: From Flagstaff, drive southeast on Forest Highway 3 (Lake Mary Road) for 20 miles to the intersection with Forest Road 90. Turn right onto FR 90 and drive 3.5 miles to the Montezuma Lodge turnoff. From there, turn right and drive 0.6 miles to the trailhead.
Vehicle Requirements: None; accessible by all vehicles
Dogs Allowed: Yes (on a leash)
USGS Maps: Mormon Lake, Mormon Mountain
Information: Peaks/Mormon Lake Ranger Districts, 928-526-0866 or www.fs.fed.us/r3/coconino

Red Mountain Trail

Coconino National Forest | Flagstaff

The old double-decker buses in London, the square in Moscow, the Coke can, Bonnie Raitt's hair, the little girl who was stalked by the Big Bad Wolf ... a lot of icons in this world are red, but in Arizona, red is an adjective that usually describes scenic rock formations, especially in Sedona and Monument Valley. Not as famous, but impressive nonetheless, is Red Mountain, which sits about 25 miles northwest of Flagstaff.

According to the U.S. Geological Survey, Red Mountain is one of several hundred cinder cones within a large volcanic field that stretches from Williams to the canyon of the Little Colorado River. The centerpiece of this hike is Red Mountain, which erupted about 740,000 years ago. By comparison, Sunset Crater, the well-known volcano just north of Flagstaff, erupted around A.D. 1050. This one is much older, but that's not what makes it unique. What's unusual about Red Mountain, which rises 1,000 feet above the surrounding landscape, is that its internal structure is exposed — like a massive geode that's been cracked in half. This one-of-a-kind trail takes you into that core, an area known as the amphitheater.

The trailhead is located just off U.S. Route 180, the highway most people take when heading to the Grand Canyon from Flagstaff. Few passersby, however, ever stop. And that's too bad, because this short hike offers not only scenery, but also a great lesson in geology. Plus, the trail is

The sweet smell of cliffrose permeates the Red Mountain Trail in August. | NICK BEREZENKO

The Red Mountain Trail gives hikers the unique opportunity to trek inside an ancient volcano. | TOM BEAN

rated Easy, so just about anybody in the car can do it.

It begins with a gradual uphill climb through a field of scattered junipers and piñon pines. For the most part, you'll be surrounded by open country, which allows for some wonderful panoramic views of the San Francisco Peaks to the northeast, as well as Red Mountain right in front of you. By the way, in addition to being easy, it's impossible to get lost on this trail. Even Mr. Magoo could find his way.

The last half-mile of the hike follows a normally dry streambed. If you look down at the sand, you'll see thousands, even millions, of black shiny granules, some of which are as big as golf balls. These granules are often mistaken for "Apache tears," which are composed of obsidian, the volcanic glass that was highly valued by ancient cultures for crafting arrowheads, knives, scrapers and other tools. But don't be fooled. What you're actually seeing are the crystals of minerals (pyroxene and amphibole) eroded from

Although there isn't a trail, the summit of Red Mountain (7,965 feet) can be accessed by an old road along the south side of the mountain, followed by some bushwhacking through the forest to the top.

the volcano. When you get into the amphitheater, take a closer look at the walls and you'll see more of these minerals embedded in the cinders. Eventually, they'll be plucked out by water and wind erosion.

Meantime, they're among the many things to explore inside the amphitheater, along with the erosional pillars known as "hoodoos" — they're similar to what you see in Bryce Canyon National Park. As you look around, remind yourself that you're actually standing *inside* an ancient volcano. It's a rare opportunity. An experience at least as impressive as standing in Red Square or next to Bonnie Raitt.

Delicate thistles go "hiking" on the wind. | SUZANNE MATHIA

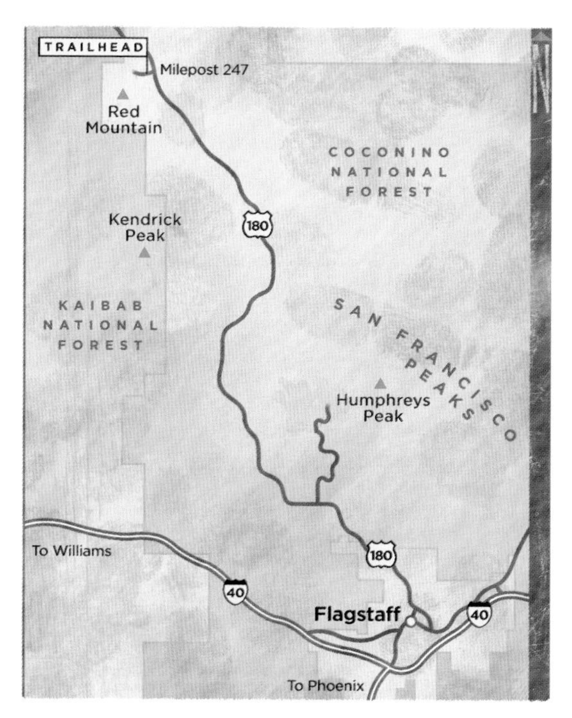

34 | TRAIL GUIDE

Length: 2.5 miles round-trip
Difficulty: Easy
Elevation: 6,745 to 7,200 feet
Trailhead GPS: N 35˚32.225', W 111˚51.474'
Directions: From Flagstaff, drive northwest on U.S. Route 180 for approximately 25 miles to a dirt road at Milepost 247 (look for the Forest Service sign that marks the Red Mountain Trail). Turn left onto the dirt road and drive about a quarter-mile to the trailhead.
Vehicle Requirements: None; accessible by all vehicles
Dogs Allowed: Yes (on a leash)
USGS Maps: Flagstaff, Ebert Mountain
Information: Peaks/Mormon Lakes Ranger Districts, 928-526-0866 or www.fs.fed.us/r3/coconino

35

San Francisco Peaks Trail

Arizona Trail | Coconino National Forest

"Few are altogether deaf to the preaching of pine trees. Their sermons on the mountains go to our hearts; and if people in general could be got into the woods, even for once, to hear the trees speak for themselves, all difficulties in the way of forest preservation would vanish."

John Muir, the renowned conservationist who wrote those words in January 1896, had strong convictions about the persuasive nature of Mother Nature. Although he never set foot on the San Francisco Peaks segment of the Arizona Trail — it wasn't even conceived until a century after his quote — he would have loved it for its accessibility. After all, the more people you can get into the woods the better, and this trail makes it easy. If you can walk across the

A grove of aspens and ferns greets hikers along the San Francisco Peaks portion of the Arizona Trail, which is a National Scenic Trail. | ROBERT STIEVE

A ponderosa pine and forest flora compete for hikers' attention. | PAUL GILL

street, you can probably handle this hike — or at least part of it. Put it on your list, and when you go, listen to the pine trees. The aspens and the ferns might have something to say, as well.

The San Francisco Peaks segment of the impressive Arizona Trail is segment No. 34 — there are 43 segments in all that make up the 819-mile trail. If you were to hike the entire Peaks segment from Schultz Pass to Cedar Ranch, you'd rack up 32.3 miles. Every mile is worthwhile, but this listing, which is unofficially dubbed the "San Francisco Peaks Trail," covers only a segment of the segment, from Aspen Corner to Forest Road 418. While you're enjoying the scenery, keep in mind that the trail you're hiking comes courtesy of the Arizona Trail Association. Its volunteers do remarkable work. And this beautiful segment, which was completed in July 2009, is no exception.

The trail begins at Aspen Corner, about three-quarters of the way up Snowbowl Road. The site is distinguished by a lush meadow surrounded

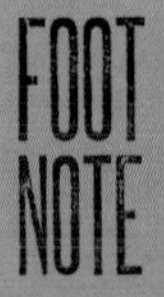

In the 1880s, biologist C. Hart Merriam used the San Francisco Peaks as the site for much of his pioneering work in how plant and animal life varies based on elevation. The result of his effort was something he called "life zones." The San Francisco Peaks, he discovered, included life zones equivalent to those in Sonora, Mexico (at the base of the mountains) and the arctic (at the summit of Humphreys Peak), as well as multiple life zones in between.

by aspens, and the meadow is separated from the small parking area by a wooden-rail fence. It's on the left. You can't miss it. For the first 10 or 15 minutes, the trail winds through a lush forest of pines and aspens. That's what the majority of the hike is like, but one of the exceptions comes before you even work up a sweat. About a quarter-mile in, the trail goes from the woods to a vast meadow, beyond which are some classic views of the San Francisco Peaks. On most hikes in Arizona, the mountains take center stage. They're a big part of this trail, too, but it's the greens of the grasses and the ferns and the aspen leaves and Muir's pine trees that stand out most. It's enough to make you think you took a wrong turn and somehow ended up in Olympic National Park.

Back in the woods, the terrain and the elevation remain constant. And so does the scenic beauty. It goes from gorgeous to gorgeous to gorgeous. Everywhere you look you're going to see something you want in your camera, including a gnarly old ponderosa about halfway in that ranks as one of the oldest and largest pine trees on the trail. If you're going to heed Muir's advice, this is the tree to listen to.

From there, the trail continues to the turnaround point at Forest Road 418. In the vicinity, there are some downed aspens surrounded by tall green grass. The trees make perfect benches for parking your butt and resting your legs. Although this trail is rated Easy, it still requires 15 miles of hiking at an elevation of around 9,000 feet. You'll be worn out by the time you get back, but if you were paying attention along the way, you'll have grown more than just tired. On this trail in particular, it seems unlikely that John Muir could have been wrong.

35 | TRAIL GUIDE

Length: 15 miles round-trip
Difficulty: Easy
Elevation: 8,928 to 9,000 feet
Trailhead GPS: N 35°19.177', W 111°43.219'
Directions: From Flagstaff, drive north on U.S. Route 180 for 7 miles to Forest Road 516 (Snowbowl Road), turn right and continue another 5.1 miles to the parking area.
Vehicle Requirements: None; accessible by all vehicles
Dogs Allowed: Yes (on a leash)
USGS Map: Humphreys Peak
Information: Peaks Ranger District, 928-526-0866 or www.fs.fed.us/r3/coconino

Uncle Jim Trail

North Rim | Grand Canyon National Park

"The North and the South." Mention that to most Americans and they'll start rattling off names like Gettysburg, Fredericksburg ... and maybe even Ken Burns. In Arizona, the North and the South are two rims of the Grand Canyon, and they're very different. Especially the hikes. On the South Rim, the trails are usually crowded — think South Kaibab and Bright Angel (see page 94). On the North, they're not. If you prefer the latter, head for the Uncle Jim Trail.

Located a few miles north of the Grand Canyon Lodge on the North Rim, this trail is named for "Uncle Jim" Owens, a game warden who reportedly killed more than 500 mountain lions in an attempt to strengthen the area's deer population. But the plan backfired. Without any predators, the deer population exploded and, as a result, thousands of deer died of starvation. Today, things are back to normal, and this trail is a good way to see it for yourself.

Like other trails on the North Rim, Uncle Jim winds through a mix of ponderosa pines, white fir, Douglas fir, blue spruce and quaking aspens, as well as ferns and grasses and pine needles. The first mile of the trail parallels the Ken Patrick Trail, so don't be confused. As you get rolling, check out the views of Roaring Springs Canyon to your right. They're incredible. After about 20 minutes, you'll come to a point where the two trails split. Stay to the right for Uncle Jim, which begins with a gentle downhill run toward a lush drainage below. Deer must love this spot.

There are many ways to see the Grand Canyon, but the views from the Uncle Jim Trail are among the best. | DAVID ELMS JR.

From the Uncle Jim Trail, hikers can see the switchbacks on the North Kaibab Trail in Roaring Springs Canyon. | DAVID ELMS JR.

Uncle Jim Owens left a legacy at the Grand Canyon beyond that of mountain lion killer. In 1906, he and others brought bison to the Kaibab Plateau. The herd's descendants now occupy House Rock Valley. Later, in 1913, President Theodore Roosevelt stayed at Owens' cabin on the North Rim. Owens served as a hunting guide for the man who not only carried a big stick, but also laid the groundwork for the creation of Grand Canyon National Park.

From there, the trail heads up the other side of the small drainage, climbing about 200 feet, and continues to another intersection on your right. This is where the Uncle Jim loop begins. The route to the right is hard to find, but if you miss it, don't worry. You'll still be on the trail. You'll just be doing the loop in a clockwise rotation. Either way is OK.

Keeping left (clockwise) you'll start catching glimpses of the Grand Canyon ahead. But even before you see it, you'll sense it. There's something about the terrain that says, "Something big is about to happen." And it does. Not far from that first glimpse, the Canyon comes into full view. Like every other perspective, this one is magnificent. Fortunately, the trail skirts the rim for most of the rest of the way to Uncle Jim Point, the apex of the loop.

You'll know you're there when you see the hitching post, which is used for the mule trains that are so popular in this national park. The point itself is a little tricky to find, but when you do, you're going to be amazed. Great views are typical on the North Rim, but the views from Uncle Jim Point are beyond words. From where you'll be standing, you'll be able to see Roaring Springs Canyon below and the San Francisco Peaks in the distance. And, if you look under your feet, literally, you'll see fossils that began their timeline more than 250 million years ago, when the point was at the bottom of a warm inland sea.

Get comfortable and enjoy the views. Although you'll have to finish the loop before it gets dark, Uncle Jim Point is a great place to sit and contemplate the merits of the two rims. They're both special, but as you'll see, the North wins easily when it comes to solitude.

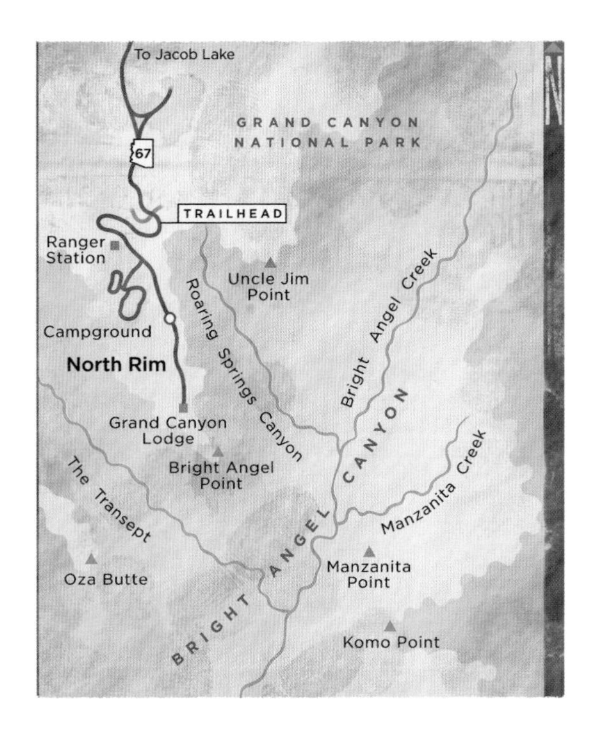

36 | TRAIL GUIDE

Length: 5 miles round-trip
Difficulty: Easy
Elevation: 8,269 to 8,427 feet
Trailhead GPS: N 36°13.052', W 112°03.329'
Directions: From the Grand Canyon Lodge on the North Rim, drive north for 2 miles to the signed right turn for the North Kaibab Trailhead. Uncle Jim shares a trailhead with the Ken Patrick Trail and a parking area with the North Kaibab Trail.
Special Consideration: National Park Service fees apply.
Vehicle Requirements: None; accessible by all vehicles
Dogs Allowed: No
USGS Map: Bright Angel Point
Information: Backcountry Office, Grand Canyon National Park, 928-638-7875 or www.nps.gov/grca

West Baldy Trail

Apache-Sitgreaves National Forests | Greer

"A saturated meadow, sun-shaped and jewel-small; a circle scarcely wider, than the trees around were tall." Robert Frost had a way with words. He also had a knack for finding Mother Nature's simple beauty. As a New Englander, most of his inspiration came from places like Vermont and New Hampshire. Had he spent a little time in Arizona, he might have found a similar muse in the magnificent White Mountains.

Like rural New England, the White Mountains are an inspiration for poets — plenty of meadows and trees and birds in the sky. It's a great place for hikers, too, especially the West Baldy Trail. For peak-baggers in Arizona, this hike is one leg of the Triple Crown — along with Humphreys Peak (see page 148) near Flagstaff and Escudilla Mountain (see page 198) near Alpine. For everybody else, it's an easy way to sample the best of the backcountry. Corkbark fir, ponderosa pines, white fir, Engelmann spruce, 5 miles of trout streams, lush meadows, black bears, deer, mountain lions and a cool wet climate (the temperature rarely tops the 70s in the summer) make this one of the most beautiful places in the Apache-Sitgreaves National Forests.

The first 2 miles of West Baldy cut through a series of wide alpine meadows and follow the West Fork of the Little Colorado River, which is dotted with beaver dams. You'll get your first glimpse of the water after about 15 minutes. Five minutes later, you'll enter the Mount Baldy Wilderness.

The first portion of the West Baldy Trail follows the West Fork of the Little Colorado River. | PAUL GILL

Aspen fleabane carpets an open meadow near the West Baldy Trail in the White Mountains of Eastern Arizona. | PAUL GILL

Looking around, you'll understand why this area was granted the ultimate protection. Of course, that also makes this one of the busiest stretches of the trail, but as the hike gets a little tougher, the crowds thin out.

After about an hour, the trail enters a thick forest dominated by spruce, fir and aspens — other than a few small meadows, the trail won't break out of the timber until the top. At the 90-minute mark, you'll cross a stream and begin a series of steep switchbacks — overall, the hike won't kill you, but the altitude and the distance do have an effect. Moving on, the

The Sitgreaves National Forest was named for Captain Lorenzo Sitgreaves, a topographical engineer for the government who conducted the first scientific expedition across Arizona in the early 1850s. Later, the U.S. Army established a series of forts in New Mexico and Arizona. To supply these forts and settlements, a military road was built linking Santa Fe, New Mexico, and Camp Verde, Arizona. Part of this road, called the General Crook Trail, runs almost the length of the Sitgreaves National Forest. The Apache National Forest is named for the Native Americans who live in this area.

trail continues its ascent to a hillside covered with fallen logs. Big logs. Lots of logs. Imagine what it would look like if Paul Bunyan had spilled a giant can of giant Lincoln Logs. That's what comes to mind, but in reality, the dead trees are the victims of bark beetles, which clobbered the area during the height of the drought in 2002 and 2003. Bears seem to like this area, too. Be on the lookout.

From there, the switches continue through an endless stretch of gorgeous evergreens, which are interspersed with boulders the size of station wagons — one looks like Abe Vigoda. Eventually, West Baldy merges with the East Baldy Trail near the White Mountain Apache Reservation boundary. The summit of Mount Baldy is on the reservation, and it's open only to tribal members. You'll be tempted to "sneak" to the top, however, this is sacred land, and it must be respected. Trespassers who ignore the boundary are subject to fines and could have their packs confiscated.

If you're a peak-bagger, here's the good news: The highest point of the ridge isn't Baldy Peak (11,403 feet), but an unnamed area (11,420 feet) on Forest Service land to the north. If you're not a peak-bagger, the news is even better: The views from the top are spectacular. It's more of Mother Nature's simple beauty. Sit back and enjoy.

That's what Robert Frost would have done.

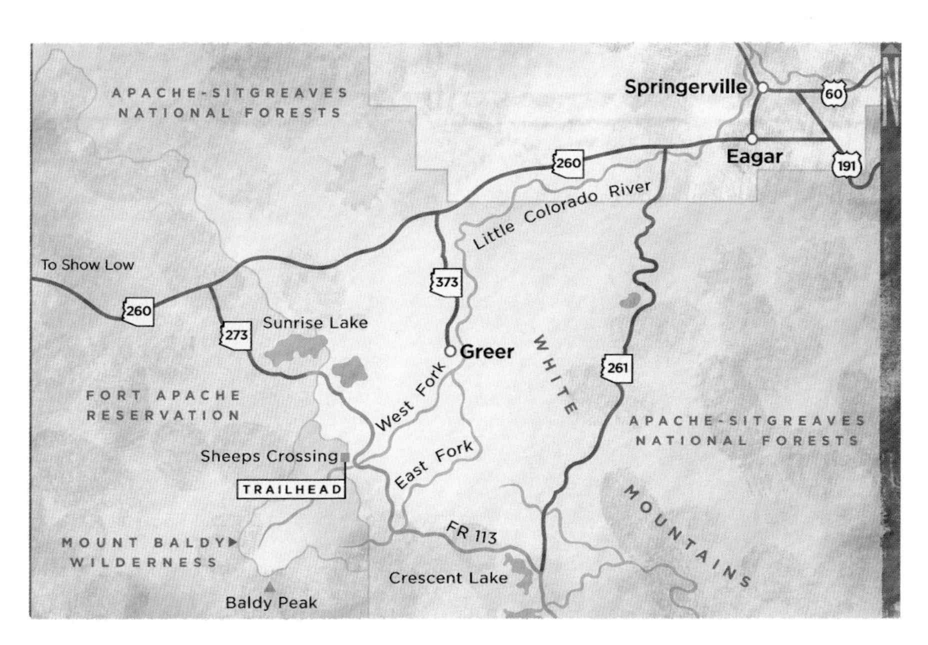

Length: 14 miles round-trip
Difficulty: Moderate
Elevation: 9,287 to 11,200 feet
Trailhead GPS: N 33°57.888', W 109°30.071'
Directions: From Eagar, drive west on State Route 260 for 18.7 miles to State Route 273, turn left and drive south for 8.6 miles to the trailhead at Sheeps Crossing.
Vehicle Requirements: None; accessible by all vehicles
Dogs Allowed: Yes (on a leash)
USGS Map: Mount Baldy
Information: Springerville Ranger District, 928-333-6200 or www.fs.fed.us/r3/asnf

38

Widforss Trail

North Rim | Grand Canyon National Park

It would be hard to single out the best hike in Arizona. There are too many 10's — just flip through the rest of this book and you'll see. Be that as it may, a solid case could be made for the Widforss Trail. It's quiet, the ecosystem is exceedingly diverse and over your left shoulder you'll see the Seventh Natural Wonder of the World. The only thing the Widforss doesn't offer is elevation gain, which is important to hikers who want to burn calories while drinking in the scenery. Still, this is a 10-mile round-tripper, so a few calories will be incinerated. Besides, if you really want a workout, the North Kaibab Trail (see page 210) is just down the road. Exercise over there, and use this trail as a reminder that it's good to be alive.

Named for Gunnar Widforss, an

The Widforss Trail, which is named for artist Gunnar Widforss, offers scenic views of Canyon landmarks, including Zoroaster Temple. | PAUL GILL

The Kaibab squirrel, which is found nowhere else in the world but the North Rim, is a shy dark animal with a bushy white tail. | BRUCE D. TAUBERT

artist who painted landscapes in the national parks of the West in the 1920s and 1930s, this relatively easy trail follows the rim of the Grand Canyon all the way to Widforss Point. A few minutes into the hike, you'll see a mounted metal box with trail guide pamphlets inside. Grab one. The guides identify points of interest at numbered sites along the first 2.5 miles of the trail. No matter how many times you've hiked this trail, or any other trail on the North Rim, you're bound to learn something from the guide.

When you're not learning, take time to enjoy the idyllic forest of Colorado blue spruce, Engelmann spruce, white fir, Douglas fir and aspens, the latter of which you'll see growing in droves where recent fires have burned. You'll be amazed at how quickly the aspens move in and shoot up when the sun isn't blocked by the towering evergreens, one of which you'll see at Site No. 8. It's not official, but this might be the biggest ponderosa pine on the trail. It's definitely impressive, and it's several hundred years old.

From the big tree, the trail meanders through the quiet forest. And that's the word you're hoping for when you're on an easy hike — *meander.*

At the height of Gunnar Widforss' career in 1929, just after his 50th birthday, the American stock market crashed, sending the artist into near obscurity and his paintings into the artistic abyss of the underappreciated. Although Widforss is considered one of the great painters of the national parks in the United States, he received limited exposure. Prior to an exhibit at the Museum of Northern Arizona in 2009-2010, there hadn't been a major Widforss exhibit since 1969, which was also held at MNA. Widforss, whose obscurity remains a paradox, is buried in the Pioneer Cemetery on the South Rim of the Grand Canyon.

As you'll see, this trail meanders for its entire length. It's the ultimate walk in the woods.

Moseying along, you'll catch glimpses of the Grand Canyon to your left. Then, after about 30 minutes, you'll come to a short side trail that leads right to the rim, from which you can see into Transept Canyon below. The Transept, which is merely a side drainage for Bright Angel Creek, isn't even part of the main canyon. Still, it's huge, which illustrates the enormity of the Seventh Natural Wonder as a whole.

The scenery stays much the same as you chalk up the miles, and after about an hour, the trail angles away from the rim and eventually leads to a lush valley, which ranks as the best part of the trail — other than the Canyon views, of course. Along this stretch, the narrow path cuts through a beautiful grove of aspens, ferns and tall grasses. The wind blows a lot on the North Rim, and this is a great place to pause and appreciate the sound. Also, if you sit still long enough, you might catch a glimpse of a Kaibab squirrel, a shy dark animal with tufted ears and a bushy white tail. Deer and turkeys are likely to cross your path, as well.

Take your time, but keep in mind the best is yet to come. Not far from the lush valley is the approach to Widforss Point. Although the trail stops short of the actual point, the views from the end of the trail are out of this world. Among other famous Canyon landmarks, you'll be able to see Isis Temple and Cheops Pyramid. You can also see Phantom Creek. Bottom line: The views are second-to-none. As you're standing there, you'll agree that few, if any, trails in Arizona have this kind of diversity and solitude. Not to mention the temples and pyramids.

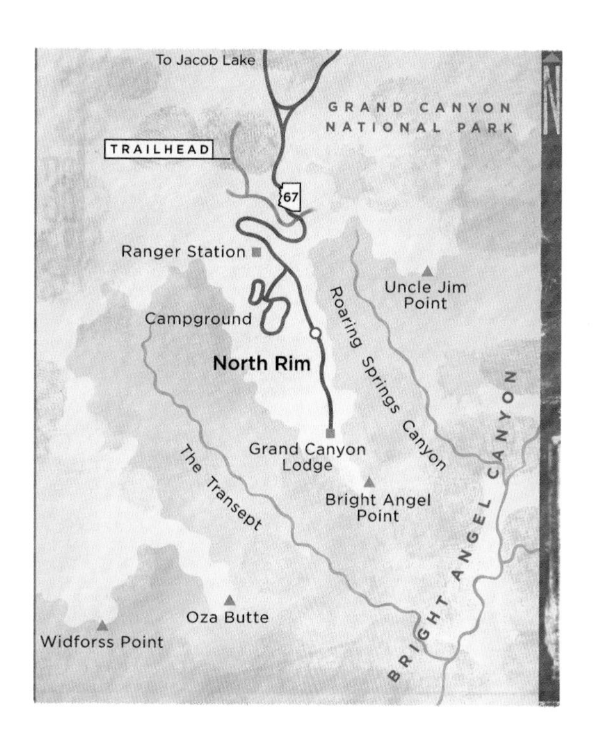

38 | TRAIL GUIDE

Length: 10 miles round-trip
Difficulty: Easy
Elevation: 8,094 to 7,811 feet
Trailhead GPS: N 36°13.427', W 112°03.899'
Directions: From the Grand Canyon Lodge on the North Rim, drive 4 miles north and turn left onto the gravel road marked with a sign for the trailhead.
Special Consideration: National Park Service fees apply.
Vehicle Requirements: None; accessible by all vehicles
Dogs Allowed: No
USGS Map: Bright Angel Point
Information: Backcountry Office, Grand Canyon National Park, 928-638-7875 or www.nps.gov/grca

Woods Canyon Lake Loop

Apache-Sitgreaves National Forests | Mogollon Rim

Hiking isn't usually something that's done in the spur of the moment. Gear, maps, vehicle requirements, trailhead directions, physical conditioning ... there's a lot to consider before hitting the trail. The Woods Canyon Lake Loop is one of the exceptions.

Naturally, a little planning is necessary, but for the most part, you could wake up on a Saturday morning, expecting to lounge around watching reruns of *This Old House*, and then think to yourself: *I've gotta get off the couch and do something.* With about as much effort as it would take to walk around the block, you could head to Woods Canyon Lake. The drive is simple and the trail is easy, requiring nothing more than a good pair of tennies, some sunscreen and a big bottle of water. That's about it. Well ... you might want to throw on some pants, too, but you get the point.

The trail begins at the Spillway Campground. It's one of the best in Arizona if you can commandeer a site. Adjacent to the campground is a small parking area, which is one option for day hikers, but the space there is limited. A better option is to drive all the way to the lake and park in the lot at the general store — it's the same lot that serves the boat landing. Parking spaces are limited at this lot, too, but you should be OK, unless it's a holiday weekend.

From the pavement, head east and follow the signs toward the amphitheater. Beyond the small structure are some random trails — there's no

Woods Canyon Lake Loop, as the name implies, takes hikers on an easy 5-mile jaunt around a small, scenic lake. | NICK BEREZENKO

Located at an elevation of 7,500 feet, Woods Canyon Lake is a cool place to hike in the summer. | NICK BEREZENKO

main trail at the outset — that wind for a few minutes to the campground. Once you get there, veer left toward the lake and look for the Spillway Dam, which is a long, narrow mound of dirt with red rocks on the lake side and green grass on the opposite slope. You'll know it when you see it.

Hop on the dirt path that crosses the dam, say hello to the many fishermen and women who will be angling from the rocks, and head for the woods, which is home to ponderosa pines, Douglas firs, Gambel oaks, bracken ferns, wild roses and this spectacular trail, which is one of the easiest and best on the Mogollon Rim.

Within minutes of entering the forest, you'll start seeing plastic blue diamonds tacked to the trees. It's a marking system that's also used on the Aker Lake Trail (see page 186) near Hannagan Meadow. Although it's virtually impossible to get lost on this trail, which parallels the shoreline for its entire length, the markers come in handy for those hikers who are directionally challenged and need some reassurance.

In addition to the blue diamonds, the forest brings an unexpected measure of solitude. Woods Canyon Lake was built for recreation, and it can feel congested at times, but the noise disappears quickly beyond the dam, and after about 10 minutes you'll come to a short side trail that leads to the water. Just beyond that junction is a tall ponderosa that's used as a nesting site by great blue herons — look for heron chicks in June.

Woods Canyon Lake, which has a surface area of approximately 50 acres and an average depth of about 25 feet, was formed by the creation of an earthen dam along Chevelon Creek. The long, narrow lake exists primarily for recreation, including fishing and boating (electric trolling motors only).

The trail continues in a counterclockwise direction with some gentle ups and downs, but the most you'll ever climb at a time is the equivalent of three flights of stairs. This is an easy trail that conjures up images of Walden Pond. It's not as serene as what Thoreau must have experienced, but by modern standards, it's pretty peaceful.

About 45 minutes into the hike, the trail winds to the end of a slough where you'll see a small creek that feeds the lake. The area around the creek is green, grassy and gorgeous, and it might be the most beautiful place on the trail.

From there, the trail climbs a series of railroad ties toward a bald eagle protection zone. Because eagles like to nest along this shoreline, the trail is detoured around the area from March 1 through August 31. The alternate route is equally scenic, and as you make your way uphill, look up in the sky — in the summer, there's a good chance of seeing the national bird.

The rest of the route continues around the lake, past the Rocky Point Trailhead and back to the boat landing. It's not a long hike, and you won't have worked up much of a sweat, but you'll be glad you rolled off the couch. Nothing against *This Old House*, but the scenery at Woods Canyon Lake is much more interesting than watching Norm Abram install a floor joist. See for yourself.

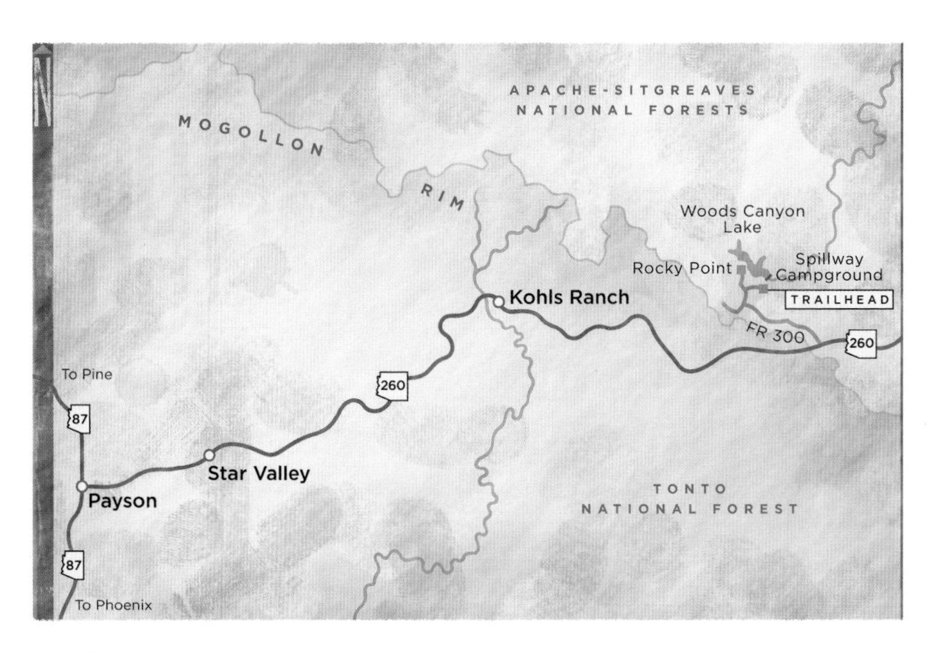

Length: 5 miles round-trip
Difficulty: Easy
Elevation: 7,500 to 7,534 feet
Trailhead GPS: N 34°20.001', W 110°56.646'
Directions: From Payson, drive east on State Route 260 past Kohls Ranch to where the road tops out on the Mogollon Rim. Turn left onto Forest Road 300 and follow the signs for 5 miles to Woods Canyon Lake. Park in the lot adjacent to the boat landing.
Vehicle Requirements: None; accessible by all vehicles
Dogs Allowed: Yes (on a leash)
USGS Map: Woods Canyon
Information: Black Mesa Ranger District, 928-535-7300 or www.fs.fed.us/r3/asnf

In fall, aspen trees are the main attraction on the Inner Basin Trail (see page 202). | TOM BEAN

FALL

Aker Lake Trail

Apache-Sitgreaves National Forests | Hannagan Meadow

Add water to just about any hike in Arizona and it's bound to get better. Not that the Aker Lake Trail needs any help. This scenic route features just about everything the White Mountains have to offer, including Douglas firs, Engelmann spruce, Colorado blue spruce, quaking aspens, grassy meadows, songbirds, raptors, elk, deer, black bears, bobcats, coyotes, squirrels, foxes, wild turkeys, spotted owls and blue grouse, among others. You might even catch a glimpse of a Mexican gray wolf.

Sunrise reflects on Aker Lake near Hannagan Meadow, which is home to mule deer, elk and the endangered Mexican gray wolf. | NICK BEREZENKO

Hikers pass through a lush conifer forest on the Aker Lake Trail. | NICK BEREZENKO

The elusive endangered species, which is the rarest subspecies of the gray wolf in the United States, was reintroduced to the area on March 29, 1998. Clearly, there's a lot to see on the Aker Lake Trail, and the lake itself is just one more thing.

The trailhead for the hike is located a few minutes from the Hannagan Meadow Campground, which is one of the best and most accessible campgrounds in Arizona. There's a parking area for day hikers, or, for those staying in the campground, the trail can be accessed between campsites No. 6 and No. 7.

Like the Woods Canyon Lake Loop (see page 180) at the western end of the Apache-Sitgreaves National Forests, this trail is marked with plastic blue diamonds. It's easy to follow and it begins with a slight descent through a gorgeous forest that will be dominated in autumn by golden aspens. One of the first things you'll notice, other than the fall leaves, is that the path is also used by deer and elk — even ungulates know a good thing when they see it. The trail is also used by mountain-bikers. In fact, the Forest Service categorizes this route as a biking trail, not a hiking trail.

The Apache National Forest and the Sitgreaves National Forest were administratively combined in 1974 and are now managed as a single unit. The forests comprise 2 million acres and feature 34 lakes (including Aker Lake) and reservoirs, as well as 680 miles of rivers and streams — more than any other national forest in the Southwest.

In the spring, summer and fall, it serves both camps, and in the winter, it even appeals to a growing number of cross-country skiers.

After a half-hour of hiking, the trail intersects a short (0.2 miles) spur trail that leads to the KP Rim Trailhead, which serves as a launch pad for some great hikes into the Blue Range Primitive Area to the east. This junction also marks the halfway point of the Aker Lake Trail.

Ten minutes later you'll arrive at a lush meadow known as Butterfly Cienega. The meadows in the White Mountains are called *cienegas*. It's a Spanish word meaning "wet, marshy areas," which are common in places like Minnesota, Michigan and Maine. In Arizona, *cienegas* are a little harder to find, but they do exist, and Butterfly Cienega is the most prominent on the trail.

Moving on, it's 71 steps across the meadow, after which you'll re-enter the woods and begin a slight uphill climb past a smaller *cienega* to an amazing stand of aspens. On a scale of 1-10, you'll give this spot a 10. Continuing south, the trail intersects a cross-country ski route. The junction can be a little confusing, but if you keep following the blue diamonds you'll make it to Aker Lake, which is pronounced "acre" and is about the size of a football field. It's not big, but it is popular with anglers. By the way, if you're thinking of strapping a fishing pole to your backpack, keep in mind that the lake is open to fly- and lure-fishing only, and any trout taken from the water must be immediately released.

The lake is also a great place to read a book, take a nap or have a picnic. Or you could pull out a pair of binoculars and look for gray wolves. Or, better yet, you could simply take off your shoes and dangle your feet in the water. That's not something you can do on every hike in Arizona.

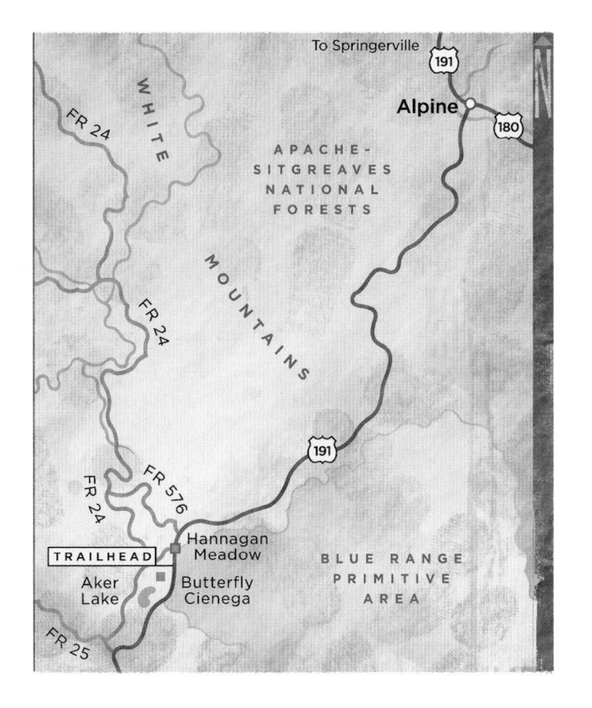

40 | TRAIL GUIDE

Length: 7 miles round-trip
Difficulty: Easy
Elevation: 9,114 to 8,836 feet
Trailhead GPS: N 33°38.027', W 109°19.732'
Directions: From Hannagan Meadow Lodge, drive south on U.S. Route 191 for a quarter-mile to the parking area on the right. The trailhead is at the south end of the lot.
Vehicle Requirements: None; accessible by all vehicles
Dogs Allowed: Yes (on a leash)
USGS Maps: Hannagan Meadow, Strayhorse
Information: Alpine Ranger District, 928-339-4384 or www.fs.fed.us/r3/asnf

41

Barbershop Trail

Coconino National Forest | Mogollon Rim

This trail is not marked by red-white-and-blue barber poles. It would be nice if it were, but it's not. Instead, this is one of the few trails in this book that can be hard to follow. Usually, all you have to do in Arizona is get to the trailhead, throw on a backpack and hit the dirt. You couldn't get lost if you wanted to. This trail is the exception. More on that later. Meantime, back to the name.

Whether it's towns, trails or back roads, Arizona has some real doozies when it comes to place-names. Gripe, Klondyke, Nothing ... they all have interesting stories behind them. And so does the Barbershop Trail, which is named for a sheepherder who once lived in the area. Apparently, he was as good at clipping his fellow herders as

The Barbershop Trail, which sits at an elevation of 7,600 feet, is one of the best for fall color. | PAUL GILL

he was at shearing sheep. In an area as beautiful as this, no doubt there was a lot of pressure to be as well-groomed and photogenic as Mother Nature.

One of the first things you'll notice when you start this hike is the postcard quality of everything around you. Unlike a lot of other Mogollon Rim hikes, which have limited ground cover, this one is lush and grassy, with ferns as high as 4 feet tall. By the looks of things, Walden Pond could be right around the corner. Instead, after about 5 minutes, you'll come to an impressive pair of ponderosas. They serve as a gateway to the trail, which, at this point, is still easy to follow.

Fall leaves and crisp air are among the many highlights of hiking on the Mogollon Rim. | PAUL GILL

After another 5 minutes, the trail passes through a gate. This is where it starts to get tricky. Cairns and tree notches mark the way, but they're not always obvious. When you're in a situation like this, don't move forward until you find the next marker. Proceed cautiously and methodically, like Harrison Ford in *Indiana Jones and the Last Crusade* — once you see where to go, take the next step.

Heading east, the trail winds down a rocky slope and into a lovely meadow. Cross the meadow and the streambed, and head up the other slope. After about 20 to 25 minutes into the hike, you'll come to another gate. Again, the trail is hard to find. Take your time and eventually you'll enter Dane Canyon. It's one of many canyons along this trail, and depending on the weather, it could have water running through it. Water, of

The present-day Buck Springs Fire Guard station consists of two cabins. The smaller cabin was built in 1932, and the larger in 1946. The cabins are still used in the summer to house fire crews.

course, attracts wildlife, which in this area includes wild turkeys, mule deer, elk and black bears. Maybe you'll get lucky and see something.

From the canyon, the trail quickly leads to a point where it merges with an old jeep road. Look for cairns and notches to the right. About 10 minutes later, you'll cross another road and finally come to a large meadow. This is the trickiest part of the trail. You'll want to head left across the meadow, which is about the size of a football field. Keep your eyes peeled for a cairn at the opposite end, alongside a forest road. Stay to the left and look for the subsequent cairns, including one that eventually marks a 90-degree turn to the right. At this point you'll be back in the woods. It's beautiful, especially when the aspens, oaks and maples are in their autumn attire, but don't let your eyes wander too much — the search for the elusive cairns continues.

The effort pays off when you come to a sign that indicates you're a half-mile from the Buck Springs cabins. The cabins mark the finish line, and like the hike itself, there are no barber poles to let you know you've arrived. Not to worry, though. Compared to the cairns, the cabins stand out like Spider Rock in Canyon de Chelly. Look around, catch your breath and gear up for the return trip, which will be much easier now that you know where you're going.

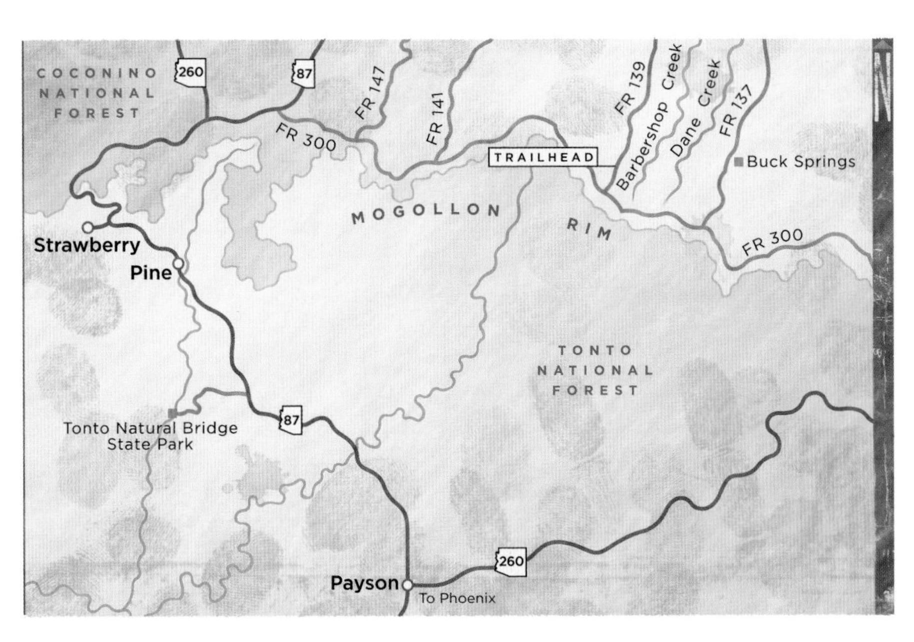

Length: 9 miles round-trip
Difficulty: Moderate
Elevation: 7,665 to 7,811 feet
Trailhead GPS: N 34°26.353', W 111°11.992'
Directions: From Payson, drive north on State Route 87 for 28.5 miles to Forest Road 300. Turn right onto FR 300 and continue 16.6 miles to Forest Road 139. Turn left onto FR 139 and continue 1.9 miles to the trailhead on the right.
Vehicle Requirements: None; accessible by all vehicles
Dogs Allowed: Yes (on a leash)
USGS Map: Dane Canyon
Information: Mogollon Rim Ranger District, 928-477-2225 or www.fs.fed.us/r3/coconino

Butterfly Trail

Coronado National Forest | Santa Catalina Mountains

Weldon Heald, a writer, artist and photographer, coined the term "sky islands" in 1967. He was referring to those mountain ranges that are isolated from one another by vast expanses of desert and grassland plains. The 70,000-square-mile sky islands region of Southeastern Arizona, southwestern New Mexico and northwestern Mexico is especially impressive. According to the Sky Island Alliance, it's home to more than half the bird species of North America, 29 bat species, at least 3,000 species of plants and 104 species of mammals. As a whole, it's an area more diverse than anywhere else in the United States, including Alaska. Think about that for a second.

There are approximately 40 sky islands in the Southwest, and the Santa Catalina Range near Tucson, which tops out at 9,157 feet, is the third highest. There are numerous hikes in the Catalinas, and throwing a dart at the map is as good a way as any of making a choice. However, when it comes to biological diversity, the Butterfly Trail might outrank them all. It's so diverse that a portion of the trail has been designated a Research Natural Area.

There are two places to pick up the trail: the Palisade Visitors Center or a trailhead 4 miles up the highway near the access road that leads to Soldier Camp. Because the facilities are better at Palisade, you'll want to start there. Among other things, the rangers stationed at the visitors

In addition to the biodiversity of the Santa Catalina Mountains, the Butterfly Trail offers tremendous distant views. | RANDY PRENTICE

Yellow columbines seem to twinkle like stars along the Butterfly Trail near Crystal Springs. | RANDY PRENTICE

center can answer any questions you might have and get you pointed in the right direction.

The trail begins at the north end of the parking lot across the road from the visitors center. You'll see a sign for the Bigelow Trail, which is where you begin — the Bigelow overlaps the Butterfly for the first 15 minutes. It's a nice stretch through ponderosa pines and Douglas firs. In some places, there are so many pine needles on the ground they actually blur the trail. Pay attention. From the point where the Butterfly and the Bigelow split, it's 5.2 miles to the Butterfly's upper trailhead. In between the two points, you'll be treated not only to evergreens, but also box elders, bigtooth maples, alligator junipers, various species of oaks and even yuccas in the drier areas.

For the first hour or so, the trail leads downhill and offers tremendous panoramic views, both east and west. Unfortunately, you'll also see the remnants of the Aspen Fire, which ravaged tens of thousands of acres in

If you look closely on this trail you might spot the wreckage of an F-86D fighter jet that crashed in 1957. It's in the canyon bottom, upstream from Novio Falls. The plane went down during the flight of three F-86D Sabre Dogs that were stationed at Davis-Monthan Air Force Base with the 15th Fighter Interceptor Squadron, two of which collided while attempting an arrow-formation. Fortunately, both pilots ejected safely. The wreckage along the Butterfly Trail is from the jet of Lieutenant Van Vliet.

the Catalinas in 2003. The trees are unliving proof of what can happen when lightning strikes or ignorant smokers toss their cigarette butts out the window.

Eventually, about halfway through the hike, you'll head into a valley thick with maples and oaks. This is probably the most beautiful part of the trail. It can be tricky to follow in places, especially where it crosses a wash at the bottom — look to your right for the retainer logs installed by the Forest Service and the cairn by the old barbed-wire fence. A little farther along, you'll hear a creek. The butterflies for which the trail is named often congregate in clusters within this moist ravine.

The rest of the route climbs gradually past an expansive garden of ferns, one of the largest ponderosa pines you'll ever see — unfortunately, another victim of the fire — and an intersection with the Crystal Springs Trail. About 3 hours after you've started the hike you'll come to an old jeep road that leads to the upper trailhead. From there, you can either hike back the way you came, or follow the Catalina Highway to the Palisade Visitors Center. Ironically, the latter option is uphill most of the way, but it's only 3 miles, compared to 5.7 miles on the trail. No one will fault you if you take the easy road, but rest assured, Weldon Heald would have opted for the woods. There's much more diversity in there.

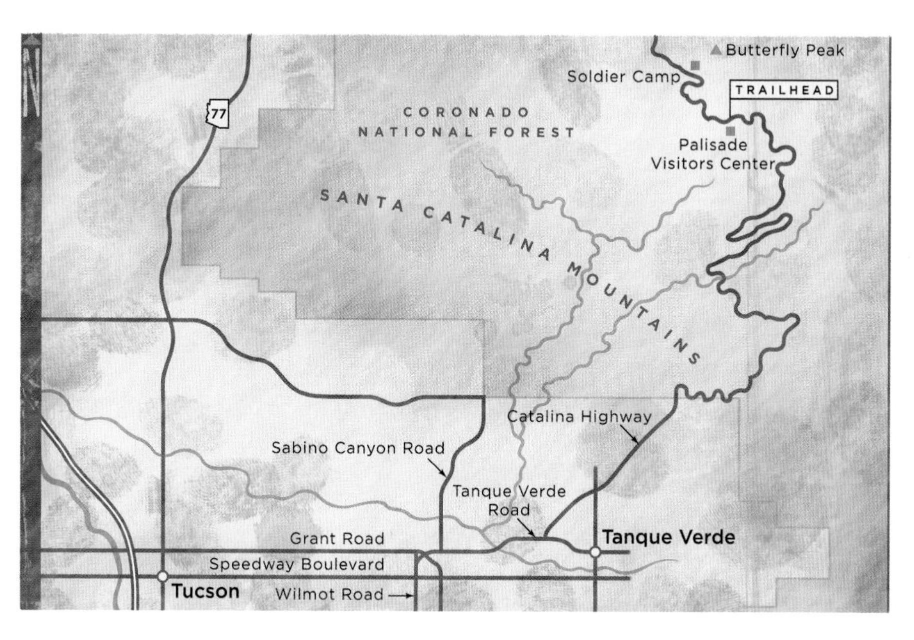

Length: 11.4 miles round-trip
Difficulty: Moderate
Elevation: 6,505 to 8,263 feet
Trailhead GPS: N 32°24.664', W 110°42.919'
Directions: From Tanque Verde Road in Tucson, drive northeast on the Catalina Highway for 4.2 miles to the Forest Service boundary and continue 19 miles to the Palisade Visitors Center.
Special Consideration: A $5 day pass is required
Vehicle Requirements: None; accessible by all vehicles
Dogs Allowed: Yes (on a leash)
USGS Map: Mount Bigelow
Information: Santa Catalina Ranger District, 520-749-8700 or www.fs.fed.us/r3/coronado

Escudilla Trail

Escudilla Wilderness | Alpine

The Escudilla Trail is unique. All hikes are unique, of course, but there isn't another hike in this book — or anywhere in the United States, for that matter — quite like this one. In addition to the aspens and firs and meadows and awe-inspiring views that make this route so special, the Escudilla Trail holds the distinction of being the only National Recreation Trail in America that's located within a designated wilderness area. It's high praise for a place that's better known for an infamous killing.

The victim was a grizzly bear, one of Arizona's last grizzlies, and its death was lamented by naturalist Aldo Leopold in *A Sand County Almanac*: "Since the beginning, time had gnawed at the basaltic hulk of Escudilla, wasting, waiting and building. Time built three things on the old mountain, a venerable aspect, a community of minor animals and plants, and a grizzly. The government trapper who took the grizzly knew he had made Escudilla safe for cows. He did not know he had toppled the spire off an edifice a-building since the morning stars sang together. ... Escudilla still hangs on the horizon, but when you see it, you no longer think of a bear. It's only a mountain now."

Mr. Leopold's point is well taken. However, this trail is definitely more enjoyable without the thought of grizzlies lurking in the aspen thickets. That said, you might see Mexican gray wolves, which were reintroduced to the area in the 1990s. Although the wolves, which can weigh up to 80

The Escudilla Trail is located near Alpine in the White Mountains, not far from where one of Arizona's last grizzlies was killed. | BRUCE D. TAUBERT

Escudilla Mountain, which gets its name from the Spanish word for "bowl," tops out at an elevation of 10,876 feet. | BRUCE D. TAUBERT

pounds, are not aggressive toward humans, they could be curious and might not retreat if they're approached. If you see one, you'll be among the few. Count yourself lucky, give it some space and move on.

The Escudilla Trail begins at Terry Flat with a gradual uphill climb through one of the most impressive aspen groves in Arizona. Because of a 23,000-acre fire that burned the area in 1951, most of the aspens are relatively small — unlike the ancient monsters that are found on the San Francisco Peaks. But size doesn't matter. These trees are as impressive as the 360-degree views from the summit.

After about 30 minutes, the aspens on your right thin out and eventually disappear. The trees that had been there were cut as part of a wildlife habitat improvement project to increase the browsing opportunities for deer. If you look to your left, you'll see that the aspens on that side of the trail have been grazed by fire, but not enough to kill them. About 5 minutes later, the meadows will open up on both sides of the trail. They're picturesque, but the wind blows hard in this open area, and without any trees to serve as a windbreaker, it can get chilly, especially in the fall.

From there, the trail winds back into the woods, but, instead of aspens, the forest is now dominated by Douglas firs, white firs, Colorado blue spruce, Engelmann spruce and ponderosa pines. Along with the vegeta-

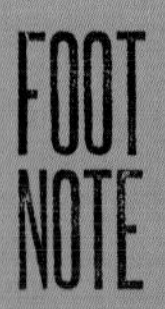

If you venture up the fire tower at the end of this trail, try to spot the two peaks that look like rabbit ears. They mark the location of the Lost Adams Diggings, the richest gold find ever in North America. According to legend, before being attacked by resident Apaches under Chief Nana, the miners found nuggets larger than robins' eggs. The story of these diggings can be read in *Black Range Tales* by James "Uncle Jimmie" McKenna. The movie *Mackenna's Gold*, starring Gregory Peck, was based on this book.

tion change, you'll also notice an elevation change. Things level off somewhat in the woods, which is another interesting aspect of this trail. Considering that this hike takes you to one of the highest peaks in Arizona, the route is comparatively easy, with most of the elevation gain occurring among the aspens. It's one more thing to love about this trail.

Moving along, the trail alternates between meadow and forest, similar to what you experience on the West Baldy Trail (see page 172), and after about an hour you'll come to a larger meadow where the Escudilla Trail intersects the Government Trail. From there, it's about a mile to the top, and about 5 minutes back to the woods. It's all trees the rest of the way — no more meadows — and as you make your way up, you're going to hear some squeaking sounds. It's the wind shifting the huge evergreens. The sound is a little startling at first, but you get used to it. That's part of the nature of Escudilla, which means "bowl" in Spanish and refers to the extinct volcanic crater that forms the mountain's summit.

Before you get there, though, there's another 10 minutes of climbing through another grove of aspens that gives way to open skies and a first glimpse of the mountain's fire tower — the highest in the state. Hikers are encouraged to climb the stairs and say hello to the attendant on duty. The wind can be unnerving as you make your way up, but the views from the lookout are worth it. On a clear day, you can see the high peaks and deep canyons of the Blue Range Primitive Area, as well as Mount Graham and the Pinaleño Mountains to the south. Some literature claims that you can even see the San Francisco Peaks from the tower, but the rangers will tell you it's never that clear. What is clear is the scenic beauty and natural diversity of this trail. Even without the grizzlies, it's truly unique.

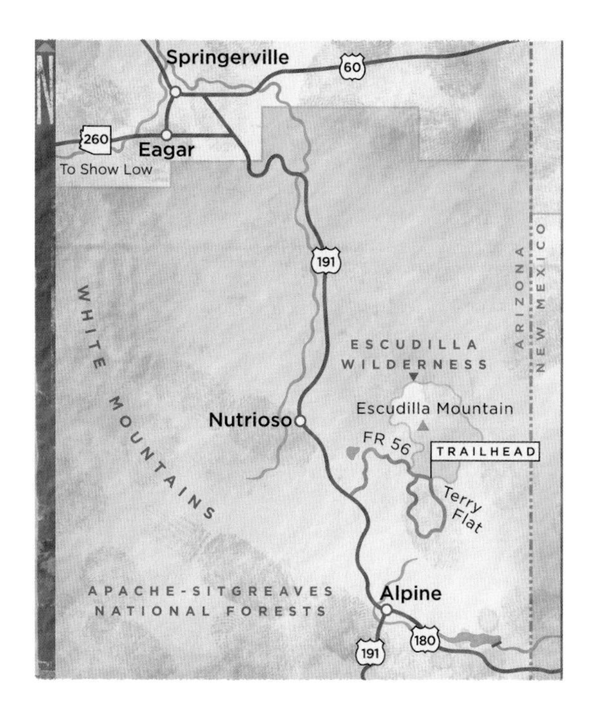

43 | TRAIL GUIDE

Length: 6 miles round-trip
Difficulty: Moderate
Elevation: 9,672 to 10,876 feet
Trailhead GPS: N 33°55.173', W 109°07.017'
Directions: From Alpine, drive north on U.S. Route 191 for 5.5 miles to Forest Road 56, turn right and continue 5 miles to the trailhead at Terry Flat.
Vehicle Requirements: None; accessible by all vehicles
Dogs Allowed: Yes (on a leash)
USGS Map: Escudilla
Information: Alpine Ranger District, 928-339-4384 or www.fs.fed.us/r3/asnf

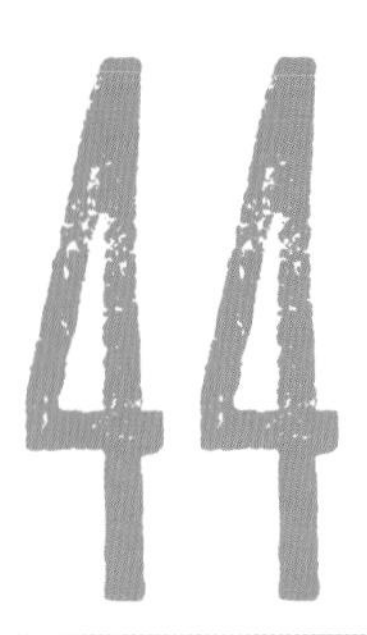

Inner Basin Trail

Coconino National Forest | Flagstaff

If you've been thinking of hiking the Matterhorn, but only have enough gas money to get to Flagstaff, head to the Inner Basin. This scenic wonder in the San Francisco Peaks is Arizona's own little version of the Alps, and the hike that takes you there is as good as it gets when autumn rolls around. It's spectacular in the spring and summer, but fall is the best time of year for exploring what was once the inside of an ancient volcano. The amber explosion of the aspens is incredible.

The trail begins at Lockett Meadow, which is home to one of the best campgrounds in the state. Are you noticing a theme here? Despite its popularity, everything about this area is picturesque and peaceful. It's grassy and green, and if you happen to be in the right place at the right time, you might even see one of the resident porcupines, elk or black bears, the latter of which have been known to stroll right through a group of picnickers without so much as a glance at their picnic baskets. Clearly, they don't work for Yogi.

From the campground, the trail climbs gradually through a forest of ponderosa pines and aspens. Although John Hancock never hiked this trail or left his mark, many others have, including Paco Lalastra Santaner, who carved his name on an innocent aspen in November 1934. The trees are covered with carvings — some old, some new, some hard to tell. The common denominator is that every one of those knife-wielding miscreants committed a crime. That includes you, "JC, (8/16/09)." Don't make the

In the fall, the Inner Basin Trail near Flagstaff is dominated by golden aspens. | NICK BEREZENKO

Although the evergreens and aspens will get most of your attention on the Inner Basin Trail, be sure to look down once in a while, too. | PAUL GILL

same mistake. Also, don't become so preoccupied with reading the graffiti that you miss the bigger picture. Instead, see the forest *and* the trees.

Among the most impressive are the seven aspens you'll see clumped together about 30 minutes into the hike. They're off to the right, just past the gate you'll pass through. A few minutes later, you'll feel the forest open up a little, and you'll come to a major intersection. To the left is the route to Schultz Pass Road. To the right is an access road to the Bear Jaw and Abineau trails. There's also an old green shed to your left with a yellow Forest Service sign that reads: "Snow-Survey Shelter, Do Not Molest." The shed is used by rangers who measure snowfall in the winter.

From this point, the Inner Basin is less than a half-mile away. But before you get there, you'll pass a log pump house that shields a well that was drilled in 1971. Because the Inner Basin provides water for the city of

Aspen trees are clonal organisms, meaning that all of the trees sprout from a common, massive root system — they're genetically identical "clones." Although the trees live for only 80 to 120 years, their root systems can live for thousands of years, making them one of the longest-living organisms in the world.

Flagstaff, there are several pump houses in the area. This one reaches a depth of 485 feet.

Beyond the well, the trail merges with an old jeep road that takes you the rest of the way. It's wide enough that you and three of your closest friends could skip side by side, à la Dorothy, the Scarecrow, the Tin Man and the Cowardly Lion. A wizard won't be waiting at the end of the trail, but Mother Nature surely will. As you'll see, there's no place like the Inner Basin. With its lush meadows and the surrounding summits of the San Francisco Peaks, you'll forget all about the Matterhorn.

An old-growth ponderosa pine sits along the Inner Basin Trail in the San Francisco Peaks near Flagstaff. | TOM BEAN

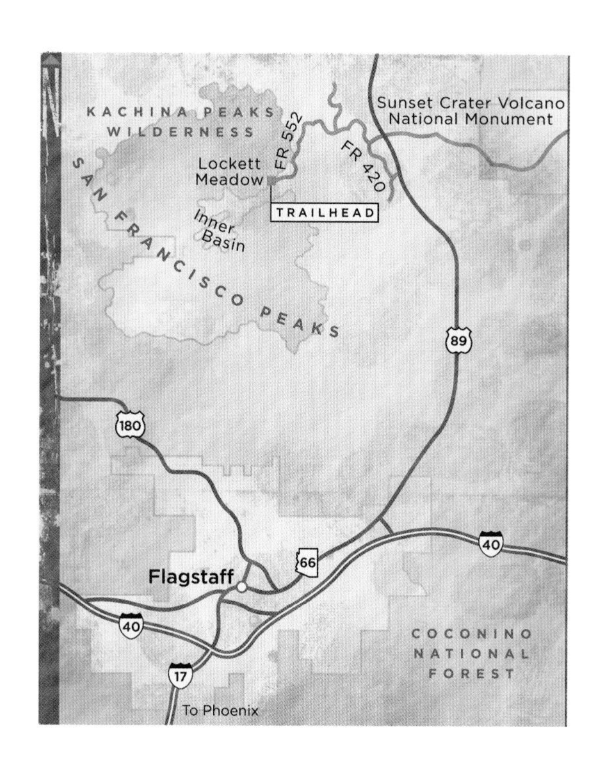

44 | TRAIL GUIDE

Length: 4 miles round-trip
Difficulty: Moderate
Elevation: 8,567 to 9,403 feet
Trailhead GPS: N 35°21.464', W 111°37.118'
Directions: From Flagstaff, drive north on U.S. Route 89 for 12 miles and turn left onto Forest Road 420, which is located across from the Sunset Crater entrance. Continue on FR 420 and follow the signs to Lockett Meadow Campground. The trailhead is well-marked.
Vehicle Requirements: None; accessible by all vehicles
Dogs Allowed: Yes (on a leash), but only below the watershed cabin
USGS Maps: Humphreys Peak, Sunset Crater West
Information: Peaks Ranger District, 928-526-0866 or www.fs.fed.us/r3/coconino

Mescal Ridge Trail

Hellsgate Wilderness | Mogollon Rim

Don't let the devilish name of this wilderness area scare you. The Mescal Ridge Trail is easy, enjoyable and it doesn't go anywhere near the netherworld. The thing is, you can't get to the Mescal Ridge Trail without first trekking for a half-mile on the Bear Flat Trail. It, too, is easy, except for that first half-mile, which climbs uphill at an incline of what feels like 45 degrees. It doesn't look that steep as you're huffing and puffing toward some breathing space up top, but on the way back down you'll get a much better perspective. Because of that hellish half-mile, this trail is given an overall rating of Moderate. After that, the rest is easy.

The name of the wilderness area, which was given by early settlers and was originally spelled "Hells Gate," comes from the turbulent water at the junction of Haigler and Tonto creeks. Together, the waterways have carved some amazing canyons in the granite rock below the Mogollon Rim. In some places, the walls rise more than 1,500 feet above the shore. The wilderness is one of Arizona's least-visited natural wonders, and the best way to experience its deep canyons and spectacular streams is to do an overnighter along the Hellsgate Trail. The hike is strenuous, and it's not for everyone, but if you're looking for more than a day hike, it's a classic. The Mescal Ridge Trail, on the other hand, is doable by just about anyone. Although you won't get wet on the trail, it does offer a bird's-eye introduction to the area. Getting started, however, can be a little confusing.

The Mescal Ridge Trail offers distant views of the Mogollon Rim and a bird's-eye view of the Hellsgate Wilderness. | NICK BEREZENKO

Agaves are a common sight along many trails in Arizona, but it's best to keep your distance because their puncture wounds are notoriously painful. | JACK DYKINGA

From the Bear Flat Trailhead, the first thing you'll need to do is cross Tonto Creek by following the concrete road that leads to a home on private property — in the springtime, this road might have water running over it. You'll see a large white sign with red letters that warns of "No Trespassing." Just before the sign, veer right and follow the creekside edge of the log fence. At the corner, you'll see a trail sign. This junction can be especially confusing. What you'll want to do is make a 90-degree turn to the left and follow the fence uphill toward an old jeep road. The wide road then climbs the hellish half-mile through a forest of mixed conifers to the wilderness boundary, and eventually leads to Bear Flat's intersection with the Mescal Ridge Trail, which veers right. That's where you're headed.

The route continues south and climbs gradually, but nothing like what's behind you. The trail itself is a mix of rock and red dirt that winds through peaceful stands of scrub oak, alligator junipers, piñon pines, agaves and manzanitas. It's best to appreciate the flora along this trail, because the fauna is less conspicuous. Nevertheless, the wilderness area around the trail is home to beavers, black bears, ringtails, mountain lions,

As you hike the Mescal Ridge Trail, keep in mind that the Hellsgate Wilderness Area is where the notorious Pleasant Valley War occurred between 1886 and 1892. The "war" was technically a feud between two rival ranching families, the Tewksburys and the Grahams. It allegedly began over some stolen horses, but quickly escalated into a violent conflict that resulted in as many as 50 deaths. The feud finally ended when the last Tewksbury killed the last Graham in the streets of Tempe.

skunks and deer. If you see something, feel free to brag about it. If you don't, you might not even notice because the panoramic views to the southeast are impressive. They're essentially the same views the Salado people had when they gazed in the same direction during the 12th and 13th centuries. Ditto for the Apaches, who later occupied this area for several centuries before being forced out by white settlers.

Back on the trail, which doesn't vary a great deal as you move along, you'll eventually come to a high point that suggests you're at the end of the hike. But you're not. Although the trail is a little hard to find at this point, look closely and you'll see that it continues downhill. A little farther on, you'll pass some old cattle fencing, and then, 15 minutes after that, you'll arrive at the Mescal Ridge Tank. The trail veers left past the tank and quickly peters out, officially marking the end of the route.

Because this is a relatively short trail, and you won't have burned up a lot of clock, you might not be in a hurry to head back down. If that's the case, Mescal Ridge is a great place to hang out, eat some lunch, take a nap or take in the views. To the southeast you can see Horse Mountain and the endless open space of Tonto National Forest, the fifth-largest national forest in the United States. Whatever you do, don't lose sight of the trail. Although the surroundings are heavenly, remember, this is Hellsgate, and the last thing you want to do is get lost in a place with a name like that.

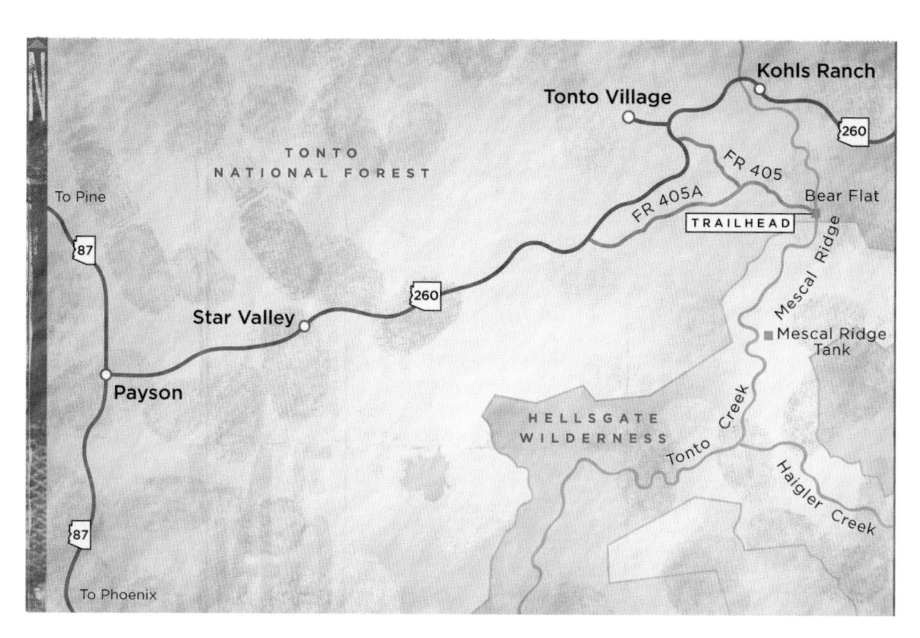

Length: 6 miles round-trip
Difficulty: Moderate
Elevation: 4,891 to 5,603 feet
Trailhead GPS: N 34°17.047', W 111°04.086'
Directions: From Payson, drive east on State Route 260 for 14 miles to Forest Road 405. Turn right onto FR 405 and drive 4.5 miles to the Bear Flat Trailhead at Tonto Crossing.
Vehicle Requirements: High-clearance recommended following rain or snow
Dogs Allowed: Yes (on a leash)
USGS Map: Promontory Butte
Information: Payson Ranger District, 928-474-7900 or www.fs.fed.us/r3/tonto

North Kaibab Trail [to Roaring Springs]

North Rim | Grand Canyon National Park

There's no shortage of great hikes on the North Rim: Widforss (see page 176), Uncle Jim (see page 168), Ken Patrick. Most, however, at least in the vicinity of the Grand Canyon Lodge, stay up top and stick to the woods. You'll get some great views of the Canyon along the way, but those trails won't take you down. The North Kaibab Trail is the exception. If you really want to experience the Seventh Natural Wonder, and see what it's like to look up for a change, this is your best option. But before you get started, you need to understand something: Even though this trail winds for 14 miles to Phantom Ranch, the farthest you should ever go on a day hike is to Roaring Springs. It's a 10-mile round-tripper, and like all Canyon hikes, the trek down is easy, but coming out ... well, the North Kaibab will kill you, but what a way to go.

The trailhead is located a couple of miles north of the lodge — it shares a parking lot with Uncle Jim and Ken Patrick. Unlike its sister to the south, the North Kaibab begins with big trees, including Douglas firs, Engelmann spruce and ponderosa pines. You'll be tempted to look up, but keep your eyes on the trail. Specifically, watch out for the mules and their unpleasant deposits. Mule trains have the right of way in the Canyon, and when you encounter one, step to the inside of the trail and await instructions from the wrangler. Generally, all you have to do is wait for them to pass. When they do, you can move on.

After about 15 minutes of switchbacking — longer if you're strolling or

The North Kaibab Trail begins at an elevation of 8,247 feet and takes hikers into Roaring Springs Canyon. | JACK DYKINGA

Hikers rub elbows with steep walls along the North Kaibab Trail above Roaring Springs. | TOM BROWNOLD

interrupted by multiple mule trains — you'll come to the Coconino Overlook. If you haven't taken the time to gaze at the wonder before you, now is a good time. What you're seeing is Roaring Springs Canyon, one of the many side canyons in the Grand Canyon. This one, however, is probably

Just below Roaring Springs is an unlikely home. It's known as the Pumphouse Residence, which is where artist and former park employee Bruce Aiken lived and painted for decades. Back in the day, you might have been lucky enough to get a cup of lemonade from one of the Aiken kids, who grew up in the home. Beginning in 1973, Aiken served as caretaker of the Roaring Springs pump house, which supplies fresh water to the park. The job came with poor pay, but Aiken loved the home and the ability to paint in the heart of the Grand Canyon. By the way, groceries and furniture had to be helicoptered in.

the most important, because water from the springs helps supply the national park's lodges and other facilities. By the way, when you're hiking back up, but still a few hundred yards below this overlook, you'll hear the voices of people standing at the overlook. There's an echo phenomenon that'll make you think there are people right behind you on the trail, but they're actually up above.

Heading downhill, you'll come to a restroom and a water fountain, followed by a 20-foot tunnel. After the tunnel, the switchbacks continue, but the trees are left behind. The makeup of the trail itself changes, too. Above the tunnel the ground is sandy. Below the tunnel, it starts getting rocky. It'll stay like that all the way to the bridge, which you'll cross about an hour into the hike. After the bridge, there's a rare uphill climb in the Canyon — rare on a downhill hike, that is. The rise takes you to the southwest wall of the canyon, where the trail follows a long ledge with steep drop-offs to your left. It's along this stretch that you'll first hear the springs. About 15 minutes later, you'll catch your first glimpse of the water.

Eventually, about 2 hours from the trailhead, you'll come to the mouth of the canyon and an intersection. To the right is the route to Cottonwood Camp and Phantom Ranch. To the left is Roaring Springs, which is 10 minutes away. At this point, you'll have dropped almost 3,000 feet in elevation. There are some picnic tables and a restroom at Roaring Springs. You should use the facilities, but you should also take off your backpack and enjoy the surroundings. When you're in Maui, you expect waterfalls like this, but not in the Grand Canyon. It's spectacular. Drink it in — figuratively, not literally — and remember: You still have 5 miles and 3,000 feet between you and the trailhead.

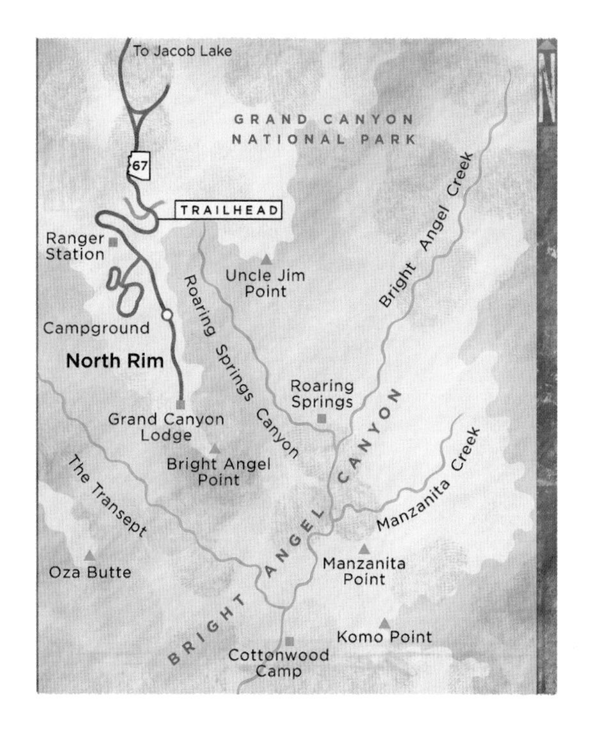

46 | TRAIL GUIDE

Length: 10 miles round-trip (to Roaring Springs)
Difficulty: Strenuous
Elevation: 8,247 to 5,221 feet
Trailhead GPS: N 36°13.020', W 112°03.406'
Directions: From the Grand Canyon Lodge on the North Rim, drive north for 2 miles to the signed right turn for the North Kaibab Trailhead.
Special Consideration: National Park Service fees apply.
Vehicle Requirements: None; accessible by all vehicles
Dogs Allowed: No
USGS Maps: Bright Angel Point, Phantom Ranch
Information: Backcountry Office, Grand Canyon National Park, 928-638-7875 or www.nps.gov/grca

47

Old Baldy Trail

Mount Wrightson Wilderness | Santa Rita Mountains

The first thing that'll come to mind when you catch your first glimpse of Mount Wrightson is, *HOLY MOLY!* Or something more graphic. Your second thought will be, *There's no way!* It's only 5.4 miles away on foot, but it's *way* up there. And it looks even farther than that.

At 9,453 feet, Mount Wrightson is the highest point in the Santa Rita Mountains. There are two trails to the top: The Super Trail (16.2 miles round-trip) and the Old Baldy Trail (10.8 miles round-trip). As you might expect, the latter, which is not to be confused with the West Baldy Trail (see page 172) in the White Mountains, is more challenging. It's also more scenic. In particular, there are more interesting plant communities on the north face of the

The Old Baldy Trail, which leads to the summit of Mount Wrightson, is one of the most difficult hikes in Southern Arizona. | RANDY PRENTICE

Clouds linger over Mount Wrightson, as seen from the Old Baldy Trail about a mile below Josephine Saddle. | RANDY PRENTICE

mountain, which is the direction Old Baldy takes.

The trail begins at the far end of Madera Canyon. Even if you're not a bird-watcher, you have to appreciate the unique nature of this place. Birders come from all around the globe hoping to spot an elegant trogon, a broad-tailed hummingbird or a yellow-billed cuckoo. Hikers come for the rocks and the trees and the challenge of conquering the summit.

From the trailhead, you'll start to feel the incline immediately, and it won't let up until you're on your way down. Within about 10 minutes, the grove of trees changes from sycamores to ponderosas. This is also where that first view of Mount Wrightson comes in. As you continue climbing, the forest gets thicker — shaggy almost — and after an hour or so, you'll come to a spectacular slope covered with ferns. There's something about ferns that seems out of place in Arizona, but there they are.

Beyond the ferns, the ponderosas start getting taller, and they're mixed with silverleaf oaks and Apache pines. They're beautiful. Equally impressive is the Josephine Saddle, which sits at 7,080 feet, 2.2 miles from the trailhead. There are some great views off to the east, but what will really catch your attention is a wooden memorial. On November 15, 1958, three young Boy Scouts, ages 12 to 16, died at this spot when they were caught in a sudden snowstorm. It's a good reminder that whenever you're hiking in Arizona, you need to check the forecast before you leave the

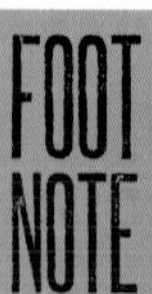

When discussing this trail, you might hear people refer to the summit as Mount Baldy or Old Baldy, which is a reference to the bald head of an Army captain who served at nearby Fort Buchanan. In 1930, the peak was officially named for William Wrightson, a local citizen who was killed by Indians.

house. Flash-flooding in the deserts and lightning and snow in the mountains can be deadly. Be smart.

From the saddle, the trail gets noticeably steeper and includes some challenging switchbacks. It's beautiful every step of the way, with brilliant green everywhere, but your legs and your lungs won't really appreciate it. If you're not breathing too hard, keep your eyes peeled for white-tailed deer, black bears and some very fat squirrels, especially around Bellows Spring, which you'll pass along the way.

After about 3 hours, you'll finally arrive at Baldy Saddle, an almost treeless place that's used as a campsite by backpackers. The summit is still about a mile away, and in places, the trail is better suited for mountain goats than day hikers. It's steep and rocky, and one misstep could ruin an otherwise perfect day. At the top of the mountain are the remains of a fire tower built in 1921. It was 12 square feet and had a work area, a kitchen and a sleeping area. A ladder led to a cupola, where an instrument called a Firefinder was located. The structure remained in use until the 1950s.

Today, all that's left of the tower is a section of its foundation, but the views are still the same. On a clear day you can see Sierra San José in Mexico, as well as several surrounding mountain ranges, including the Rincons, the Galiuros and the Chiricahuas. Also, to the west, you'll see the Smithsonian Institution's Whipple Observatory, which looks like a misplaced igloo at the top of Mount Hopkins. To some observers, the telescope is an eyesore. To others, it's a scientific marvel. To the hikers who make it to the top of Mount Wrightson, it's just one more thing to look down on as they think to themselves: *HOLY MOLY! I made it to the top.*

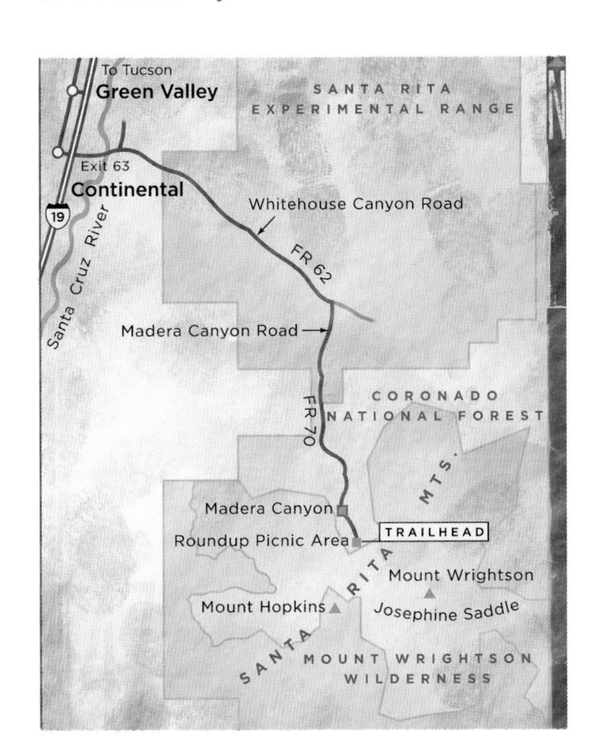

47 | TRAIL GUIDE

Length: 10.8 miles round-trip
Difficulty: Strenuous
Elevation: 5,403 to 9,453 feet
Trailhead GPS: N 31°42.944', W 110°52.483'
Directions: From Tucson, drive south on Interstate 19 for 24 miles to Continental Road (Exit 63). Turn left and drive 1 mile to Whitehouse Canyon Road. From there, turn right and follow the signs for 5.6 miles to the Madera Canyon Recreation Area. The trailhead is near the Roundup Picnic Area.
Special Consideration: A $5 parking pass is required.
Vehicle Requirements: None; accessible by all vehicles
Dogs Allowed: Yes (on a leash)
USGS Map: Mount Wrightson
Information: Nogales Ranger District, 520-281-2296 or www.fs.fed.us/r3/coronado

48

Parsons Trail

Sycamore Canyon Wilderness | Coconino National Forest

You probably won't see any parsons along this trail. Priests, rabbis, nuns ... none of them. In fact, there's a good chance you won't see anybody. Unlike the Red Rock/Secret Mountain Wilderness to the east, the Sycamore Canyon Wilderness is relatively unknown. But don't let the lack of foot traffic give you the wrong idea. This trail explores one of the most spectacular riparian areas in the state.

The centerpiece of the wilderness, which was established in 1935 and ranks as one of the first areas to be protected in Arizona, is the canyon itself. In all, it winds for more than 20 miles along Sycamore Creek, a spectacular waterway that might be even more impressive than the canyon. It's the water, of course, that gives life to the area's wide array of vegetation, including cottonwoods, sycamores, Arizona walnuts, scrub oaks, manzanitas, hackberry, desert honeysuckles and wild grapes. And there's wildlife, too. Golden eagles, mountain lions, bobcats, badgers, great blue herons and black bears all call this place home. Most of these creatures are elusive, but you never know.

The trail begins with a steep drop of about 200 feet from the rim to the canyon floor. After that, things remain mostly level all the way to the spring, which is just shy of 4 miles away. The first thing you'll notice along the bottom of the canyon is the makeup of the trail. It's smooth and sandy and easy on the feet, and in the fall it'll be covered with autumn leaves. You'll also notice the water. You'll hear it initially, then, after about

The Parsons Trail leads hikers into one of the most spectacular riparian areas in Arizona. | DEREK VON BRIESEN

Fall leaves are just one of the highlights along the Parsons Trail. | DAVID MUENCH

10 minutes, you'll come to the first of many small pools. The first pool even has a miniwaterfall.

Another thing you'll notice is the quiet. It's so still that even the leaves can be heard hitting the ground. Literally. The trail continues like this for about a half-hour, at which point you'll come to the first of several creek

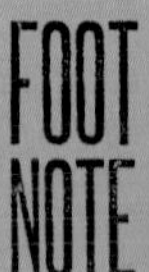

An old cowboy line shack built in 1931 for rancher Nick Perkins is nestled into the canyon wall along Sycamore Creek. Backpackers often use the shack, which is listed on the National Register of Historic Places, as a shelter while passing through. Cabin rules, which were inscribed by Perkins in the cupboard door, request that guests replenish the water jugs and firewood for future travelers. Don't disappoint him.

crossings. Although this hike is rated Easy, it does require some boulder-hopping and some concentration. All of the crossings are marked with cairns, but some can be hard to find. This area floods regularly, which obliterates many of the markers. Look closely and you'll see where to go.

After a couple more creek-crossings and about 15 minutes of hiking, the largest pool along the hike will come into view. To get there, you'll have to detour off the trail about 100 feet, but the extra steps are mandatory. Compared to every other water hole along the way, this one is Lake Superior. It's gorgeous. And completely unexpected. It varies in size, depending on the weather, but in general, it's at least as big as an Olympic-sized swimming pool. What makes it even more impressive is the wall of rock that surrounds it. The cliffs of Sycamore Canyon are a unique mix of dark columnar basalt, buff-colored limestone and red sandstone. At the big pool, the red rocks are dominant. Both in scale and color. Have your camera ready.

Beyond this point, the trail climbs away from the creek and skirts a canyon wall for about 20 minutes. Then, it's back and forth across the creek until you come to Parsons Spring, which is marked by an old sign. There's a pool at the spring, too, but it's not impressive. Not in size, anyway. Nevertheless, the spring itself pumps out more than 5,000 gallons per minute. It's water that turns an otherwise dry streambed into a perennial creek. As you're sitting there eating your trail mix, you'll be wondering why more people don't visit this idyllic place. Although there aren't any parsons or priests in the area, the hike evokes all kinds of spiritualism, and for those who worship Mother Nature, it's a religious experience.

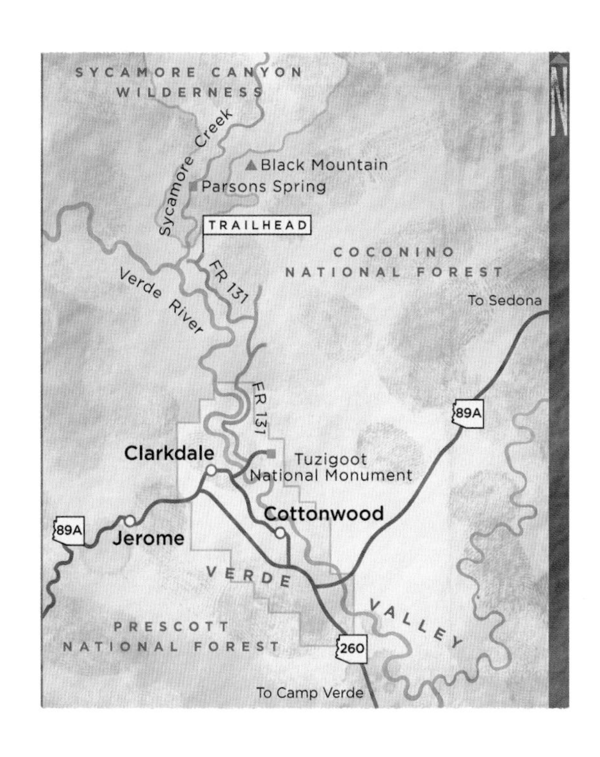

48 | TRAIL GUIDE

Length: 7.4 miles round-trip
Difficulty: Easy
Elevation: 3,775 to 3,671 feet
Trailhead GPS: N 34°51.837', W 112°04.143'
Directions: From Cottonwood, drive northwest on Main Street (State Route 260) and follow the signs toward the turnoff for Tuzigoot National Monument. Turn right onto Tuzigoot Road, continue across the Verde River bridge and turn left onto Forest Road 131 (Sycamore Canyon Road). From there, it's 11 miles to the trailhead.
Vehicle Requirements: High-clearance vehicle is required
Dogs Allowed: Yes (on a leash)
USGS Maps: Sycamore Basin, Clarkdale
Information: Red Rock Ranger District, 928-282-4119 or www.fs.fed.us/r3/coconino

Sterling Pass Trail

Oak Creek Canyon | Sedona

You're either going up or you're going down on the Sterling Pass Trail. There's no in between. No middle ground, no plateaus, no real respites. No matter, it's still one of the best hikes in Oak Creek Canyon. And that's saying something, because the canyon, which includes the world-famous Red Rock/Secret Mountain Wilderness, of which this trail is a part, is loaded with great hikes: A.B. Young, West Fork (see page 68), Loy Canyon (see page 48) ... there aren't any bad options in this vicinity, but Sterling Pass ranks near the top because it's easy to find, moderate to climb and extreme in terms of scenic beauty.

Named for a local settler — as so many hikes in Arizona are — the Sterling Pass Trail is located about 10 feet from the side of the highway, and you need to be careful when you pile out of the car. Although State Route 89A through Oak Creek Canyon is one of the most spectacular drives in the world, there are still people who feel a need to race down the road as if they were Jimmie Johnson. Again, be careful. Once you're on the trail, the engine noises will quickly disappear and be replaced by the idyllic sounds of the birds and the breeze.

The trail kicks off with a series of short switchbacks, nothing too strenuous, that lead to an unnamed drainage. At this point, the trail is a little hard to see, but if you cross the wash you'll see a cairn marking the route. The trail is easy to follow the rest of the way, which allows you to

The eye-catching reds of big tooth maple leaves litter the forest in Sterling Canyon. | LARRY LINDAHL

focus on the Mother Nature — in particular, the vermilion- and buff-colored cliffs, mesas and spires that make Sedona one of the state's scenic wonders. It's second only to the Grand Canyon in terms of recognition around the world.

Among the rock formations is the trail's namesake, Sterling Pass, which is a short saddle that sits between Wilson Mountain and the Mogollon Rim. It also separates Oak Creek Canyon and Sterling Canyon. The saddle is easy to see, but to get there, you'll first have to climb 1,100 feet through a forest of ponderosas, junipers and manzanitas. About 10 minutes into the hike you'll come to some dead trees. They're the victims of a fire, and because the trail cuts right through the burn area, you'll get an up-close look at what can happen to the woods when fire restrictions are ignored.

Afternoon sun dapples the Sterling Pass Trail just north of Sedona. | LARRY LINDAHL

Even with the burnouts, the trail is worthwhile, and after about 20 minutes you'll begin the switchbacks up to Sterling Pass. The climb offers a good workout, like Camelback Mountain (see page 60) in Phoenix, and the switches get tighter near the top. Enjoy the views from above, because you're about to start switching again. Immediately. This time, zigzagging downhill into Sterling Canyon. The terrain is similar to what you saw coming up, but the views are more open, more panoramic.

Eventually, after 2.4 miles, you'll come to the end of the route, where the trail meets the Vultee Arch Trail, which is yet another one of the area's great hikes. In fact, if you were to hike every trail in the Red Rock/Secret Mountain Wilderness, you'd realize that it's impossible to make a wrong turn. Every hike is worth taking. Sterling Pass just happens to be one of the few that were chosen for this book.

Vultee Arch, which can be reached via the Sterling Pass Trail, is named for Gerard "Jerry" and Sylvia Vultee. In 1938, the couple flew their Stinson aircraft through the area, and after encountering an unexpected snowstorm, crashed about a mile from the arch. Both passengers were killed instantly. Gerard was a well-known aviation pioneer and the head of the Vultee Aircraft Corp. in California. The arch, which bears a large bronze plaque commemorating the couple, stands against the far north wall of Sterling Canyon and is surrounded by thick, heavy brush.

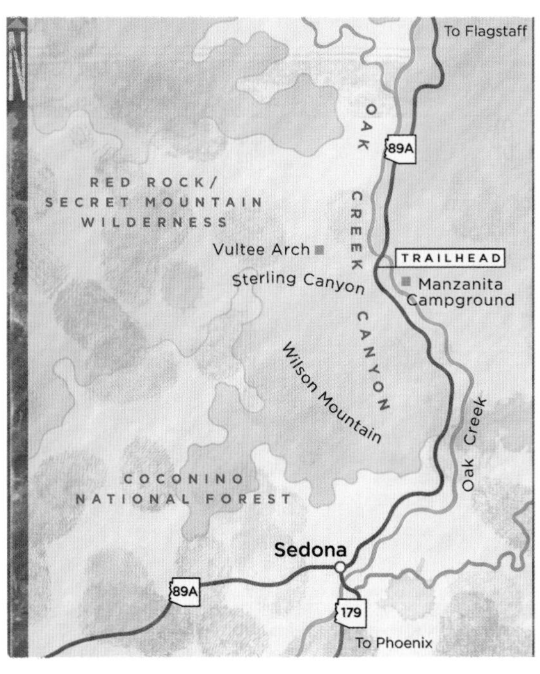

49 | TRAIL GUIDE

Length: 4.8 miles round-trip
Difficulty: Moderate
Elevation: 4,849 to 5,950 feet
Trailhead GPS: N 34°56.198', W 111°44.829'
Directions: From Sedona, drive north on State Route 89A for 6 miles to the trailhead on the west side of the road, about a half-mile north of milepost 380. Park in one of the roadside pullouts across from Manzanita Campground.
Special Consideration: A $5 Red Rock parking pass is required.
Vehicle Requirements: None; accessible by all vehicles
Dogs Allowed: Yes (on a leash)
USGS Maps: Munds Park, Wilson Mountain
Information: Red Rock Ranger District, 928-282-4119 or www.fs.fed.us/r3/coconino

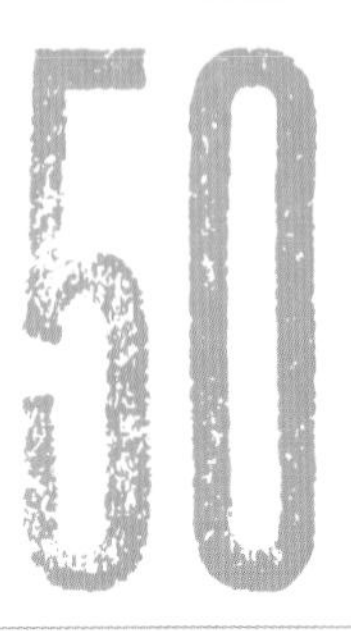

Sycamore Rim Trail

Kaibab National Forest | Williams

People like to poke fun at the 1970s. Bell-bottoms, shag carpeting, 8-tracks ... they were outta sight back then, but now, they're just punch lines. Of course, the '70s produced some real classics, too, including the Sycamore Rim Trail, which was proposed in 1975 to protect a unique environment of ponds, streams, cliffs and deep canyons. People liked the idea, and the route was finally cleared and marked in 1979. Since then, the Sycamore Rim Trail has become an easy way to get a good look at Arizona's second-largest canyon.

From the trailhead, the dirt path crosses a small meadow and enters the forest. The trail, which isn't identified as such, is a loop. You'll be going clockwise toward Dow Spring and an old sawmill site. The remains of the mill

The Sycamore Rim Trail features many small pools, some of which are crowded with lily pads. | TOM BEAN

The Sycamore Rim Trail in the Kaibab National Forest is an easy way to explore Arizona's second-largest canyon. | TOM BEAN

serve as a reminder that you're in timber country. Although this particular sawmill ceased operation in 1920, logging continues in the forest. Just beyond the mill, you'll get some terrific views of the San Francisco Peaks to the northeast. Then, after about 45 minutes, you'll see the first of many small pools.

Reminiscent of something you might come across in Maine or Minnesota, the pools are crowded with lily pads and cattails, and surrounded by lush green grass. No doubt these are prime locations for spotting wildlife — deer and elk in particular. After about an hour, the trail intersects an old logging road. It's a little confusing, but you'll want to stay right and look for a giant cairn. Eventually, the trail goes left and reaches the rim of Sycamore Canyon and the border of the Sycamore Canyon Wilderness Area.

While exploring the Sycamore Canyon Wilderness Area, keep your eye out for what forest rangers call the "camp robber," the infamous ringtail, sometimes called a ringtail cat. Interestingly, Arizona's official state mammal isn't a member of the cat family, but belongs to the raccoon family and looks like a combination of a fox and a raccoon. Ringtails can also be distinguished from raccoons by their somewhat slender bodies and more agile movements.

Technically, the trail never enters the wilderness, but the views for the next hour or so, about 3 miles in all, are nothing but wilderness. It's a beautiful canyon, one that grows from a small ditch to a big wow! It gets bigger and better all the way to Vista Point, which is the halfway mark of the trail. The views, as the name suggests, are worth stopping for. From there, it's back into the woods, past the normally dry Sycamore Falls, and on to the Pomeroy Tanks. These perennial pools support a population of small fish and quench the thirst of area ungulates.

The next landmark is just beyond the intersection with the Overland Trail. At the junction, you'll see a field — at least as big as Lambeau — of jagged volcanic rocks. Making your way across the terrain can be a little tricky, so be careful. On the other side, you'll begin a 500-foot ascent of KA Hill, which sits at an elevation of 7,287 feet. The climb is the only section of the trail that'll get your heart pumping. Still, it's nothing too strenuous.

From the top, the trail winds for another 20 minutes back to the trailhead, but don't be in a rush to leave. KA Hill is the highest point of the hike, and the 360-degree views from the summit include Garland Prairie, the San Francisco Peaks and the Mogollon Rim. As you'll see, the vistas are spectacular, or as they used to say in the '70s, they're outta sight.

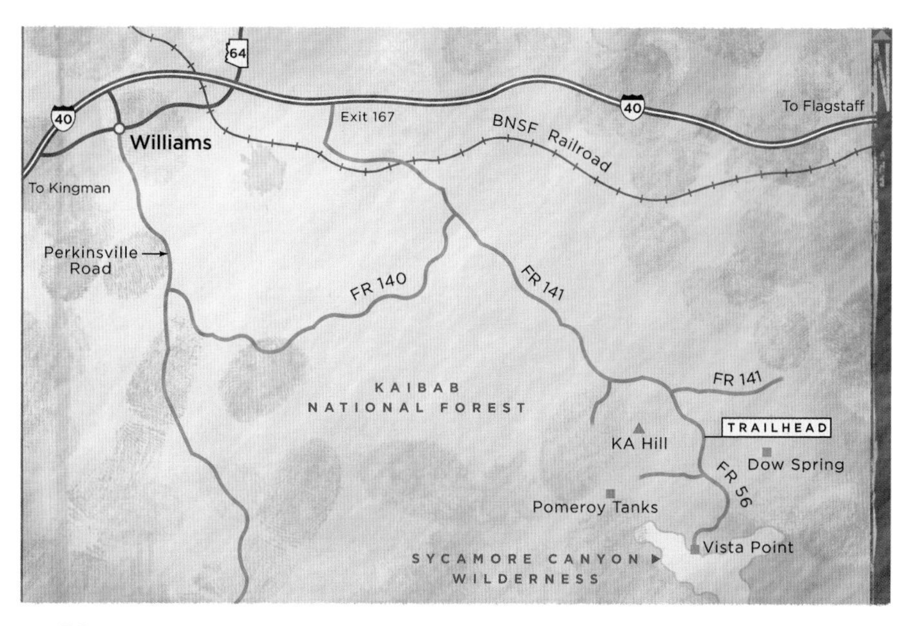

Length: 11-mile loop
Difficulty: Easy
Elevation: 6,721 to 7,287 feet
Trailhead GPS: N 35°09.623', W 112°00.034'
Directions: From Flagstaff, drive west on Interstate 40 for approximately 25 miles to the Garland Prairie Boulevard exit (Exit 167), turn left and drive south on Forest Road 141 for approximately 12 miles to Forest Road 56. Turn right onto FR 56 and continue 1.5 miles to the trailhead parking area on the left.
Vehicle Requirements: None; accessible by all vehicles
Dogs Allowed: Yes (on a leash)
USGS Maps: Bill Williams Mountain, Garland Prairie, Sycamore Point
Information: Williams Ranger District, 928-635-5600 or www.fs.fed.us/r3/kai

Weatherford Trail [to Doyle Saddle]

Coconino National Forest | Flagstaff

It's hard to imagine driving a Model T up the slopes of Fremont Peak, but that's what John Weatherford had in mind in the 1920s when he constructed an eponymous toll road to the upper reaches of the San Francisco Peaks. It was an ambitious undertaking that was ultimately undermined by the Great Depression. Fortunately, he had better luck with his hotel in Flagstaff. Today, the Hotel Weatherford (he liked his name) is one of the best places to stay, and his toll road, as it turns out, has turned into one of the best trails in Arizona, despite being threatened by the devastating Schultz Fire in June 2010.

The easy-to-follow route, which no longer resembles a road, begins at Schultz Tank and climbs gradually through an open grove of ponderosas to an intersection with the Kachina Trail.

Flowers and aspens dot a lush hillside in the San Francisco Peaks. | MOREY K. MILBRADT

During the fall, lucky hikers might hear the bugling sounds of bull elks. | C.K. LORENZ

When you get there, look around. Although the trail is rated Moderate for difficulty, it's rated extreme for beauty. The pines, the aspens, the meadows, the mountains ... no wonder Weatherford chose this route. It looks like something you'd see on a John Denver album cover.

Continuing uphill, the trail enters the Kachina Peaks Wilderness Area. From this point, it's about 4 miles to Doyle Saddle, the turnaround point for this listing. The saddle is named for Allen Doyle, a hunting guide who had a camp in the peaks in the late 19th century. The saddle makes an ideal turnaround, but don't rush to get there. The scenery only gets better as you climb toward the sky.

Beyond Doyle Saddle, the Weatherford Trail eventually leads to the Fremont-Agassiz saddle. On the saddle, you'll find the rusty remains of Allen Doyle's tourist camp, which are strewn about. Doyle was known as Arizona's foremost hunting guide in the early 19th century; however, there aren't many accounts of his colorful career. What we do know is that Doyle shared many adventures with famous author Zane Grey and, unknowingly, inspired many of the characters in Grey's Western novels.

Just past the wilderness boundary, you'll skirt the ridge of a shaded canyon on your right. As you look across to the opposite slope, you'll see a kaleidoscope of greens. The colors of the trees are stunning. And so are the golden aspens you'll encounter along the trail in the fall. Sadly, hundreds of reprobates have carved their initials into the trees. Some of the etchings are recent, and some date back decades to the Basque sheepherders who worked the area. If you get an undisciplined urge, remember, you're not a Basque sheepherder. You're a hiker. They were bored. You won't be. Leave the trees alone.

Moving on, the trail becomes a series of gradual switchbacks and the vegetation changes from ponderosas and aspens to alpine species including corkbark firs and Englemann spruce. It's in this area that you might see bears, turkeys, blue grouse and Clarks nutcrackers, a type of jay. The best encounter, however, will be made with your ears, not your eyes — listen for the bugling of bull elk as they lumber through the woods in search of willing partners.

Wildlife notwithstanding, you'll eventually get to a point where the forest opens up and views of the peaks steal the show. There's one place in particular, just before you make the turn into the final switchback, where you'll want to turn around. "Whoa" is what you'll whisper.

From there, it's a quick hop to the top of the saddle. If it isn't stormy, settle in and enjoy the views. On a clear day, you can see all the way to Oak Creek Canyon. And in the fall, the leaves will be changing color, making the Inner Basin even more beautiful than normal. And best of all, it's free. Despite John Weatherford's best-laid plans.

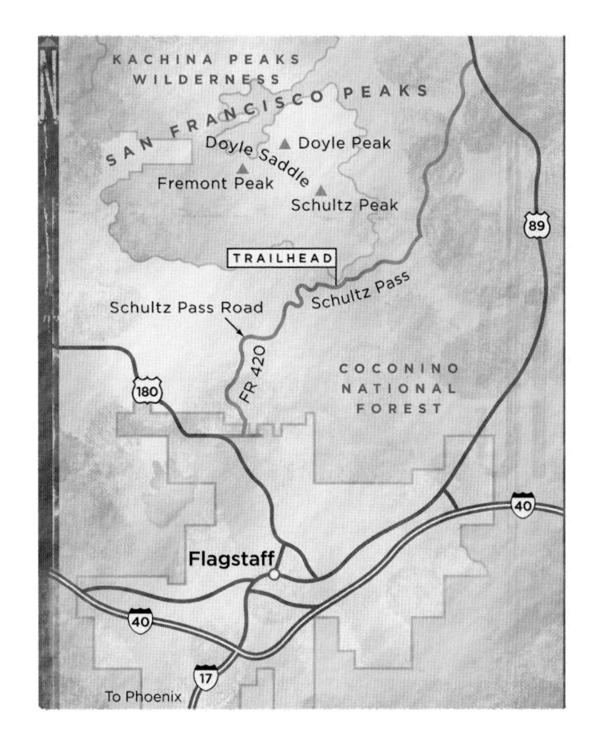

51 | TRAIL GUIDE

Length: 14.8 miles round-trip (to Doyle Saddle)
Elevation: 8,103 to 11,344 feet
Difficulty: Moderate
Trailhead GPS: N 35°17.178', W 111°37.627'
Directions: From Flagstaff, drive north on U.S. Route 180 for 2 miles to Forest Road 420 (Schultz Pass Road). Turn right onto FR 420 and continue past the end of the pavement for approximately 5.5 miles to the trailhead, which is on the right side of the road. FR 420 is closed in the winter because of snow.
Vehicle Requirements: None; accessible by all vehicles
Dogs Allowed: Yes (on a leash)
USGS Map: Humphreys Peak
Information: Peaks Ranger District, 928-526-0866 or www.fs.fed.us/r3/coconino

West Fork Black River Trail

Apache-Sitgreaves National Forests | Greer

In most cases, when you mix black and white you get gray. In Eastern Arizona, it's different. When you combine the Black River with the White Mountains you end up with green — leafy, grassy, lush green. And in the fall, when football weather rolls around, you'll find gold on the palette, too. Green and gold, like the Green Bay Packers, but the tickets are easier to come by. And they're free. All you have to do for this hike is make one of the most scenic drives in Arizona — the White Mountain Scenic Road, which is a National Scenic Byway — park the car and hit the trail. This is the last hike in the book, but it's one of the best.

The trail begins with a warning about keeping your food "secured and unavailable to all wildlife at all times." It sets the tone for what you'll immediately recognize as an incredible adventure in the great outdoors. The warning sign applies to bears, which are attracted by odors and will eat just about anything. Although it might seem generous to leave a Hostess Twinkie or a PB&J lying around for the wildlife, it's just the opposite. Once bears lose their fear of humans, they either have to be relocated or destroyed. Follow the rules and keep your junk food in the car.

From the trailhead, the hike crosses a short grassy area and enters the woods, which is made up primarily of ponderosa pines, white pines, Engelmann spruce, Colorado blue spruce, Douglas firs and quaking aspens — in autumn, it's the aspens that provide the gold in the palette.

Like the Aker Lake Trail (see page 186), the West Fork was built for

The well-maintained West Fork Black River Trail is popular with hikers and mountain-bikers. | PAUL MARKOW

The West Fork Black River Trail is ideal for anyone looking for an idyllic walk in the woods. | PAUL MARKOW

mountain-bikers, as well as hikers, and there's a good chance you'll encounter a set of wheels at some point along the way. Another thing you'll run into are black rubber bars, which are embedded in the trail. They're similar to railroad ties, and they're there to carry runoff away from the trail and prevent erosion. Not only is this one of the most scenic trails in Arizona, it's also one of the best maintained.

About 10 minutes into the hike you'll cross a wooden landing, and just beyond that you'll arrive at Neck Tank, which sits in the first of two meadows on the trail. In the White Mountains, the meadows are called *cienegas*. It's a Spanish word that means "wet, marshy areas." In any language, these areas are great places to see elk and mule deer, especially around dawn and dusk. Other wildlife in the area include the aforementioned bears, along with coyotes, mountain lions and Mexican gray wolves.

From the tank, the trail veers left and continues on a level course

The West Fork of the Black River is one of the few places in Arizona where the Apache trout (*Oncorhynchus apache*) exists. It's the state fish, and it's one of only two trout species native to Arizona — the other is the Gila trout (*Oncorhynchus gilae*). Once on the verge of extinction, the Apache trout is making a comeback in much of its historic range in the White Mountains after decades of cooperative protection and recovery efforts. The Apache trout is found nowhere else in the world.

through a verdant forest to the second *cienega*. At the far end of the meadow you'll see a stone structure. From a distance, it's hard to tell what it is, but if you trek over to it, you'll see that it's the remains of an old fireplace. Backpackers use it as a campsite, and what a site it is.

Not far from the second meadow, the trail arrives at the ridge of the canyon that shelters the West Fork of the Black River. From there, the trail begins its descent to the water, and about 10 minutes later you'll arrive at a wooden footbridge that spans a rockslide. If you listen closely, you might hear water trickling beneath the rocks. If not, no worries. The river is just minutes away.

If you grew up on the Mississippi, the Black River won't look like a river. It'll look more like a brook or a creek or a tributary of something bigger. It is a river, though, and it gives life to a montane riparian zone that's reminiscent of something you'd see in Washington or Montana. The water is dark and cold and supports a healthy population of trout; along the river, the handiwork of the resident beavers can be seen in the form of gnawed willows and aspens; and all around is the color green — leafy, grassy, lush green. It's gorgeous, and it's the last thing you'd expect from a mixture of black and white.

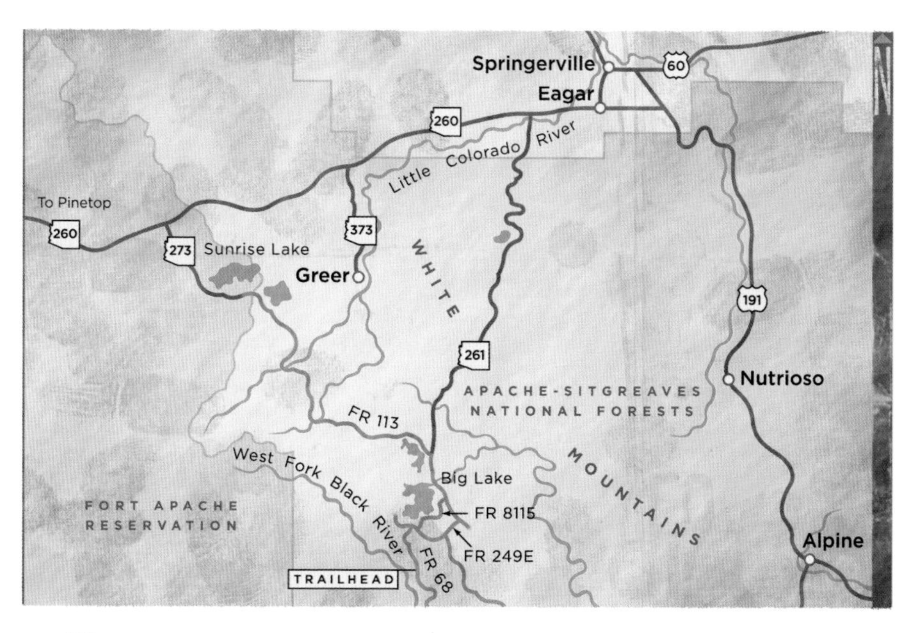

Length: 6 miles round-trip
Difficulty: Easy
Elevation: 9,106 to 8,681 feet
Trailhead GPS: N 33°51.251', W 109°25.502'
Directions: From Pinetop, drive east on State Route 260 for 22 miles to State Route 273, turn right and drive south for 18.5 miles to Forest Road 8115 (follow the signs to Big Lake). Turn right onto FR 8115 and drive 2.5 miles to Forest Road 249E. Turn right onto FR 249E and drive 0.2 miles to Forest Road 68, turn left and continue 1.2 miles to the trailhead on the right.
Vehicle Requirements: None; accessible by all vehicles
Dogs Allowed: Yes (on a leash)
USGS Map: Big Lake
Information: Springerville Ranger District, 928-333-6200 or www.fs.fed.us/r3/asnf